INTERMEDIATE
LEVEL 3

Choral
Connections

Treble Voices

 **Glencoe**
McGraw-Hill

New York, New York   Columbus, Ohio   Woodland Hills, California   Peoria, Illinois

Cover Photo: Peter Samuels Photography

Glencoe/McGraw-Hill

A Division of The **McGraw·Hill** *Companies*

Send all inquiries to
Glencoe/McGraw-Hill
21600 Oxnard Street, Suite 500
Woodland Hills, CA 91367

ISBN 0-02-655617-0 (Student's Edition)
ISBN 0-02-655618-9 (Teacher's Wraparound Edition)

Printed in the United States of America.

1 2 3 4 5 6 7 8 9   045   04 03 02 01 00 99 98

Meet the Authors

Mollie G. Tower, Senior Author
As Coordinator of Choral and General Music of the Austin Independent School District for 21 years, Mollie Tower was recently nominated as "Administrator of the Year." She is very active in international, national, regional, and state music educators' organizations. Ms. Tower was contributing author, consultant, and reviewer for the elementary textbook programs, *Share the Music* and *Music and You*. Senior author of *Música para todos, Primary and Intermediate Dual Language Handbooks for Music Teachers*, she has also written and consulted for many other publications. A longtime advocate for music education, Mollie is a popular clinician who conducts workshops across the country.

Milton Pullen
Professor of Music and Director of Choirs
After attending Texas A & I University where he acquired a Bachelor of Music Education in voice, Milton Pullen attended the University of Houston, where in 1976 he received a Master of Music in conducting. He has taught at the middle and high school levels for 24 years and for the last nine years has taught at the university level. He is now Professor of Music and Director of Choirs at Pepperdine University in Malibu, California.

Ken Steele
Director of Choral Activities
Ken Steele has taught secondary choral music for 23 years, having directed choirs at the middle school and high school levels. He received the Bachelor of Music degree from Stetson University in DeLand, Florida, and went on to the University of Texas in Austin to earn the Master of Music in Choral Literature and Conducting in 1971, studying with Dr. Morris J. Beachy. A member of Texas Music Educators Association, Texas Choral Directors Association, Texas Music Adjudicators Association, and a lifetime member of the American Choral Directors Association, he is currently the director of choral activities at L. C. Anderson High School, in Austin, Texas.

Gloria J. Stephens
Director of Choral Activities
With 25 years of teaching experience, Gloria Stephens is presently the Director of Choral Activities at Ryan High School in Denton, Texas. Mrs. Stephens earned her Bachelor of Music Education and Master of Music Education degrees from the University of North Texas in Denton. She has also done postgraduate work at Texas Woman's University in Denton, the University of Texas at Arlington, and Westminster Choir college in Princeton, New Jersey.

Consulting Author

Dr. Susan Snyder has taught all levels of vocal music over the last 25 years. She holds a B.S. in music education from the University of Connecticut and an M.A. from Montclair State College. She holds a Ph.D. in curriculum and instruction from the University of Connecticut and advanced professional certificates from Memphis State University and the University of Minnesota. Teaching at Hunter College and City University of New York, Dr. Snyder was coordinating author of the elementary music program, *Share the Music*, and a consultant on *Music and You*. She has published many articles on music education and integrated curriculum and is an active clinician, master teacher, and guest conductor.

Consultants

Choral Music
Stephan P. Barnicle
Choir Director
Simsbury High School
Simsbury, Connecticut

Vocal Development, Music Literacy
Katherine Saltzer Hickey, D.M.A.
University of California at Los Angeles
Los Angeles, California
Choir Director
Pacific Chorale Children's Choruses
Irvine, California

Music History
Dr. Kermit Peters
University of Nebraska at Omaha
College of Fine Arts
Department of Music
Omaha, Nebraska

Contributors/Teacher Reviewers

Dr. Anton Armstrong
Music Director and Conductor, St. Olaf Choir
St. Olaf College
Northfield, Minnesota

Jeanne Julseth-Heinrich
Choir Director
James Madison Middle School
Appleton, Wisconsin

Caroline Lyon
Ethnomusicologist
University of Texas at Austin
Austin, Texas

Caroline Minear
Supervisor
Orange County School District
Orlando, Florida

Judy Roberts
Choir Director
Central Junior High School
Moore, Oklahoma

Dr. A. Byron Smith
Choir Director
Lincoln High School
Tallahassee, Florida

Table of Contents

ADDITIONAL PERFORMANCE SELECTIONS

CHORAL MUSIC TERMS

Preparatory Material

Notes and Note Values

1 Whole Note

equals

2 Half Notes

equal

4 Quarter Notes

equal

8 Eighth Notes

equal

16 Sixteenth Notes

Rests and Rest Values

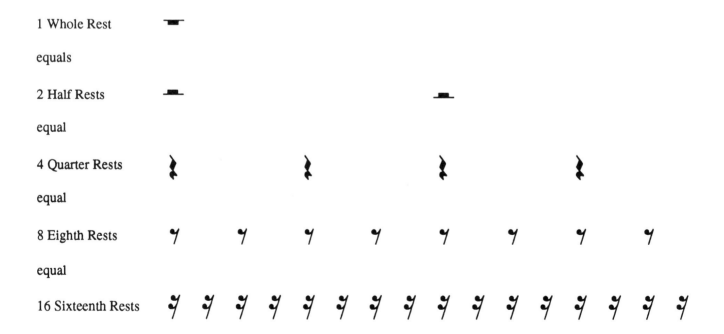

1 Whole Rest

equals

2 Half Rests

equal

4 Quarter Rests

equal

8 Eighth Rests

equal

16 Sixteenth Rests

Rhythm Challenge in 4/4 Meter

Directions: Accurately count and/or perform the following rhythms without stopping!

Asymmetric Meter

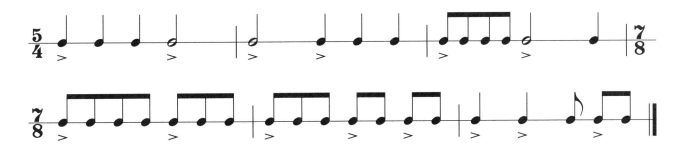

Rhythm Challenge in 6/8 Meter

Directions: Accurately count and/or perform the following rhythms without stopping!

Breathing Mechanics

Singing well requires good breath control. Support for singing comes from correct use of the breathing mechanism. Deep, controlled breathing is needed to sustain long phrases in one breath. Also, correct breathing will support higher, more difficult passages.

Posture
Posture is very important in breath support.
- Keep your body relaxed, but your backbone straight.
- To stretch your back: Bend over and slowly roll your back upward until you are standing straight again. Do this several times.
- Hold your rib cage high, but keep your shoulders low and relaxed.
- Facing front, keep your head level. Imagine you are suspended by a string attached to the very top of your head.
- When you stand, keep your knees relaxed, but do not "lock" them by pushing them all the way back. Keep your feet slightly apart.
- When you sit, keep both feet flat on the floor and sit forward on the edge of your chair.

Inhaling
- Expand the lungs out and down, pushing the diaphragm muscle down.
- Inhale silently without gasping or making any other noise.
- Keep the throat and neck muscles relaxed to maintain a feeling of space in the back of the mouth (picture a reverse megaphone).
- Imagine taking a cool sip of air through a straw, lifting the soft palate.
- Expand your entire waistline, keeping the chest high, and the shoulders relaxed, feeling the breath low in the body.

Breath Control
To help you develop breath control do the following:
- Hold one finger about six inches from your mouth imagining that your finger is a birthday candle. Now blow out a steady stream of air to blow out the flame of the candle.

Summary

STANDING
Feet slightly apart, one
slightly forward
Knees relaxed
Backbone straight
Rib cage high
Shoulders low
Head level

SITTING
Feet on the floor
Sit on edge of chair
Backbone straight
Rib cage high
Shoulders low
Head level

Solfège and Hand Signs

Solfège is a system designed to match notes on the staff with specific interval relationships. Hand signs provide additional reinforcement of the pitch relationships.

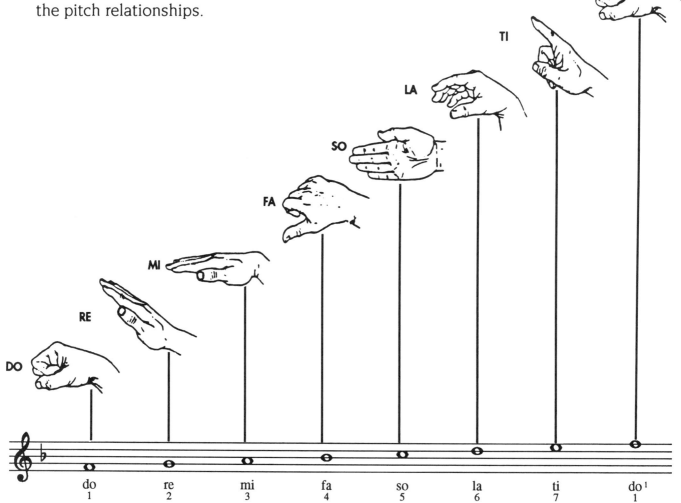

Frequently Found Intervals

An interval is the distance between two notes.

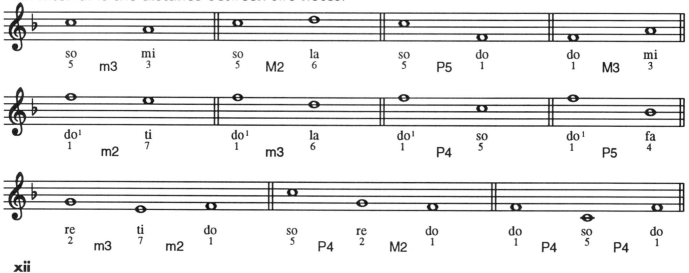

Pitch Challenge

Directions: Accurately sing each measure on solfège using hand signs and without stopping! During the measure of rest, look ahead to the next challenge.

Lessons

LESSON 1

The Rainbow Comes and Goes

COMPOSER: *Lois Land*
TEXT: *William Wordsworth (1770–1850)*

CHORAL MUSIC TERMS

andante

breath support

intervals

major second

major sixth

major third

octave

perfect fifth

perfect fourth

posture

rhythm

VOICING

SSA

PERFORMANCE STYLE

Andante

A cappella

FOCUS

- Read and clap rhythms.
- Use correct posture and breath support.
- Aurally and visually identify and sing intervals of a major second, major third, perfect fourth, perfect fifth, major sixth, and an octave.

Warming Up

Body Warm-Up

Use your imagination to do this warm-up. Stand, pretending a birthday cake is balanced on each shoulder. Be sure the cakes don't fall to the ground as you walk carefully around the room. You are demonstrating the correct posture for singing.

Rhythm Drill

Speak and clap each line separately. Then divide into sections and perform all three lines at the same time. Strive for precision and accuracy.

Vocal Warm-Up

Sing this pattern on *loo*. Be sure to follow the dynamic markings to help connect the pitches.

Loo   loo   loo   loo   loo.

Sight-Singing

Sight-sing this exercise using solfège and hand signs or numbers. For variety, read the exercise in reverse after you have mastered reading it in the usual manner. Starting with the end pitch, sing the pitches going to the left until you reach the beginning pitch. Identify the intervals of major third, perfect fourth, perfect fifth, and an octave. Which are easy to sing in tune? Which are difficult?

Singing: "The Rainbow Comes and Goes"

A piano tuner is a technician who tunes a piano. By playing two pitches at the same time that are a fourth apart, the technician is able to tell whether the strings need tightening or loosening.

When you read music, the notes tell you how far apart the sounds are. This distance is called an interval. Just like the technician, you need to know what the interval sounds like to decide whether your pitch is in tune, or needs adjustment. When you use your voice as an instrument, you are your own technician.

Now turn to the music for "The Rainbow Comes and Goes" on page 4.

HOW DID YOU DO?

You have begun to learn how to "play your voice." Think about your preparation and performance of "The Rainbow Comes and Goes."

1. Define how good posture and good breath support are related. Can you have one without the other? Why or why not?

2. How would you describe your ability to perform rhythms? Demonstrate by clapping one line of the Rhythm Drill, first alone, then in a trio.

3. Describe an interval, then tell the difference between a major second, major third, perfect fourth, perfect fifth, major sixth, and an octave.

4. Working with a partner, arrange for one of you to sing the first pitch of an interval, in the sight-singing exercise; then point to the interval. Your partner will sing the second pitch to complete the interval. Both of you check the accuracy of the second pitch, adjusting it until it is correct. Switch roles after several intervals.

5. What did you like about performing the piece "The Rainbow Comes and Goes"? Tell what you would change if you had the chance.

The Rainbow Comes and Goes

Lois Land
William Wordsworth

SSA, U.I.L. Sight Reading Selection for Class AAA (SSA)

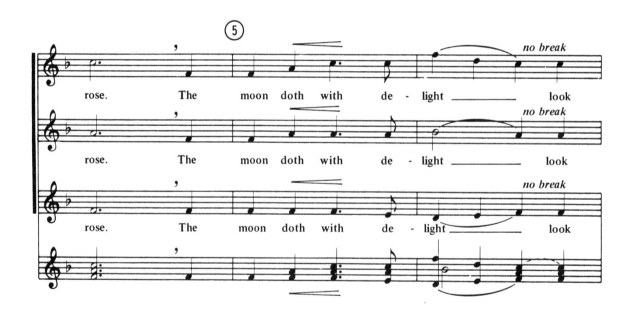

LESSON 2

Behold, a Tiny Baby!

Thirteenth Century Plainsong
ARRANGER: *Mary Lynn Lightfoot*

CHORAL MUSIC TERMS

independent singing

melismatic

minor tonality

syllabic

VOICING

SA

PERFORMANCE STYLE

With growing intensity
Accompanied by piano

FOCUS

- Read and sing in minor tonality.
- Identify and sing melismatic and syllabic use of text.
- Sing in two independent parts.

Warming Up

Body Warm-Ups

Do these exercises mirroring your teacher or a classmate. Warming up your body will help you produce a relaxed, full sound.

- Neck rolls: With a very, very loose and relaxed neck, slowly roll your head from side to side.
- Shoulder rolls: Very slowly and deliberately roll both shoulders forward five times, then backward five times.
- Head massage with shoulders: Pull shoulders up until they touch the bottom of your ears. Hold for a count of five, then quickly release the shoulders. Do this five times.
- Back massages: Massage the back of the person to your right. Then turn around and have them return the favor.

Vocal Warm-Up

Sing this example on *no*. First sing a separate *no* for each pitch, then sing the whole pattern on one *no*. Which way is syllabic, and which is melismatic? Repeat using *nay, nee, nie,* and *noo*. Keep your jaw relaxed as you form pure vowel sounds.

Sight-Singing

Sight-sing this exercise using solfège and hand signs or numbers. What is the tonal center, and what will you call it? First sight-sing the two lines separately, then sing them together. Tune the intervals carefully. Can you think of a text that would make this a melismatic passage? Now think of a different text that would be syllabic.

 ## Singing: "Behold, a Tiny Baby!"

The text of a song can be *syllabic* or *melismatic*. Syllabic text provides one syllable for each pitch. There will be a syllable in the music under each notehead. Melismatic text provides one syllable which is held for over many pitches. You can find this easily in the music, because there is only one syllable in the text, and the notes have a slur connecting them.

Now turn to "Behold, a Tiny Baby!" on page 9 and find examples of syllabic and melismatic use of text.

HOW DID YOU DO?

? ? ?

You have increased your knowledge and skills during this lesson. Think about your preparation and performance of "Behold, a Tiny Baby!"

1. Name the tonal center of "Behold, a Tiny Baby!" and sing the first two phrases using solfège and hand signs or numbers to demonstrate your reading ability in this key.

2. Sing the Sight-Singing exercise with a classmate. How well can you hold your part when there are two different parts being sung? What is easy? What needs more work?

3. Tell the difference between melismatic and syllabic use of text, then sing one of each to demonstrate.

4. Describe your performance of "Behold, a Tiny Baby!" Tell what was good first, then what could use more work. Give examples to support your thoughts. What do you think you should work on next to improve?

5. Now describe the ensemble's performance.

Behold, a Tiny Baby!

Mary Lynn Lightfoot
Quoting Veni Emmanuel, Thirteenth Century Plainsong

Two-part Chorus and Piano*
M. L. L.

Duration: approx. 3:03
*Also available for SATB (H327) and Three-part Mixed (15/1028).

Reproduced by permission. Permit # 275772.

thee, O Is - ra - el!

Part II: *mp* 22

Be - hold ____ a ti-ny ba - by! Be -

hold ____ a ti-ny child! Be - hold ____ him in a

Part I: *mp*

man - ger, so peace - ful and ___ so mild! The

an - gels sang his glo - ry! The shep - herds saw the

sign; that bless - ed light which guid - ed them to the

ho - ly child_ di - vine. Sing glo-ri - a!

Sing glo-ri-

glo - ry! The shep - herds saw the sign; that
na - tions, bind

bless - ed light which guid - ed them to the ho - ly child _ di -
peo - ples in one heart _ and mind. _

mf

vine. Re - joice! Re - joice! Em - man - u -
Sing glo-ri-a! Sing glo-ri-a!
Sing glo-ri - a, glo-ri-a! Em - man - u -

HERITAGE MUSIC PRESS A DIVISION OF THE LORENZ CORPORATION • BOX 802 • DAYTON, OH 45401-0802

Whispering Pine

COMPOSER: *Eugene Butler*
TEXT: *David Davenport*

CHORAL MUSIC TERMS

altered tones

flat

sharp

3/4 meter

tonic chord

tonic triad

tuning

VOICING

SSA

PERFORMANCE STYLE

Liltingly
Accompanied by piano

FOCUS

- Read rhythms in 3/4 meter.
- Identify, read, and sing pitches of the tonic triad.
- Tune chord tones in three parts, including altered tones.

Warming Up

Rhythm Drill

Speak and clap the following rhythms, one line at a time. Then, in three groups, clap all three lines together. Notice the crescendo over the last four measures.

Vocal Warm-Up

Sing this exercise on *loo*. Move up by half steps on the repeats. Feel the tone high in the "mask of the face." Use correct breathing techniques for a steady stream of air under the tone as you sing. The pitches *so, mi,* and *do* make a major triad.

Loo, loo loo loo loo.

Sight-Singing

Notice the altered tone, E♭. Call it *te* instead of *ti*. First all sight-sing each part separately, then divide into three voice parts and sing them together. Sing this exercise slowly, tuning each chord before moving on to the next.

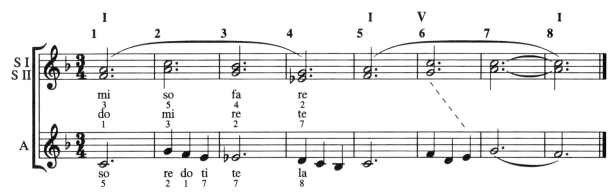

 Singing: "Whispering Pine"

The most important tones in most melodies are those of the tonic triad—*do, mi,* and *so.* In the key of F, these are:

Sing these pitches as a partner points to them in random order. Keep going until you can hear the sound inside your head before you sing it.

Now choose one pitch for each section of the ensemble to sing. You are making a chord singing all the tones at once. On a signal, change to the pitch of the section to your right. Keep changing and tuning the chords.

Now turn to the music for "Whispering Pine" on page 18.

HOW DID YOU DO?

When you understand the musical concepts within a piece of music, you can make good judgments about how to perform it. Think about your preparation and performance of "Whispering Pine."

1. Tell what the meter of the piece is and what the numbers mean. Clap one line of the Rhythm Drill to show how well you read in this meter.

2. Sing pitches of the tonic triad as a partner points to them in random order. Which intervals are easy to sing? Which are more difficult?

3. Sing measures 5–13 of "Whispering Pine" in a small group, tuning the chords.

4. How well can you sing chord tones when there are other parts being sung? Is it easier by yourself, or with your whole section singing? What might you do to improve this skill?

Whispering Pine

Eugene Butler
David N. Davenport

SSA Accompanied

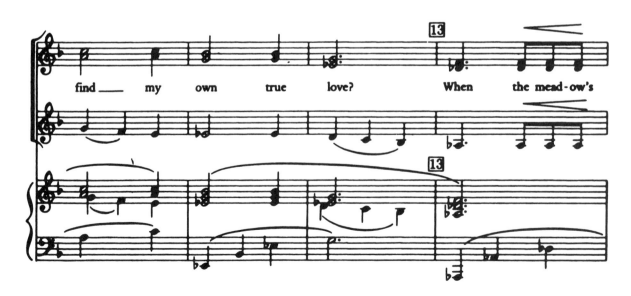

Af - ter the cold of win - ter drear

Will he ap - pear, will he ap - pear?

Will he ap - pear, O whis - per - ing pine?

Joseph's Lullaby

COMPOSER: *Russell Schulz-Widmar*
TEXT: *Fred Pratt Green*

CHORAL MUSIC TERMS

choral blend

diction

fermata

intonation

legato style

tone quality

VOICING

Three-part choir

PERFORMANCE STYLE

Gently moving
Accompanied by organ or keyboard

FOCUS

- Identify and sing using characteristics of choral blend.
- Sing in a legato style.
- Sight-sing using solfège and hand signs or numbers in F major.

Warming Up

Vocal Warm-Up

Sing this Warm-Up using solfège and hand signs or numbers. Hold the tied notes to their full value, slowly raising hands and arms from the center of the body up and out. Next, in three parts, each begin one measure after the other. Hold the *fermata* until all parts get there, then continue to the end together.

Sight-Singing

Identify the solfège syllables, then sight-sing in three parts. Listen for tuning and balance. Notice the division of the soprano part in measure 10. Use a legato style.

 ## Singing: "Joseph's Lullaby"

Think about the lullabies you have heard in the past. Many of them have the characteristics of successful choral blend (tone quality, diction, and intonation). Many lullabies you have probably heard are of a gentle, soothing nature. Yet others, such as African lullabies, often have a lively, bouncing nature.

Look at the music for "Joseph's Lullaby" on page 25 and decide whether this piece is soothing or lively.

Now sing the music for "Joseph's Lullaby."

HOW DID YOU DO? Were you able to tell the kind of performance the composer had in mind by looking at the music for the piece? Think about your preparation and performance of "Joseph's Lullaby."
1. Did you sing legato? Did the choir? How do you know?
2. Sing from measure 77 to the end of "Joseph's Lullaby" with two classmates demonstrating blended sound.

3. Tell the three characteristics of a blended sound.
4. Can you sight-sing in F major? What pitches or intervals are the most difficult to sing in tune?
5. What did you do well in this lesson? What do you still need to improve?

For Karl

Joseph's Lullaby

Russell Schulz-Widmar
Fred Pratt Green

Three-part Choir (or Choirs)
Any Combination with Organ Accompaniment

*The indications Solo and Ped. apply when this music is performed on the organ.

* The soloist should be at the same voice range as the chorus.

Joseph's Lullaby

little son, So that trav - 'lers pass - ing by

little son, So that trav - 'lers pass - ing by

little son, So that trav - 'lers pass - ing by

Think of home and has - ten on: Lul - la - by,

Think of home and has - ten on: Lul - la -

Think of home and has - ten on: Lul - la -

Lul - la - by, Think of home and has - ten on.

by, Lul - la - by home and has - ten on.

by, Lul - la - by home and has - ten on.

Solo

mp

Ped.

Joseph's Lullaby

Welcome Now in Peace

Israeli Folk Song
ARRANGER: Judith Herrington

CHORAL MUSIC TERMS
chord

major

minor

vowels

VOICING
Two-part

PERFORMANCE STYLE
Expressively
Accompanied by piano

FOCUS
- Form vowels correctly for effective diction while singing.
- Identify, read, and sing in D minor.
- Visually and aurally distinguish major and minor chords.

Warming Up

Vocal Warm-Ups

Sing these Warm-Ups first using solfège and hand signs or numbers, then on the syllable provided. Can you tell which is in major or minor? Work for focused vowels throughout. Move up or down by half steps as you repeat.

Neh   neh   nah nah neh   nah noh nah noh   neh. _____

Neh   neh   nah nah neh   nah noh nah noh   neh. _____

Sight-Singing

Clap the rhythm, then sight-sing this exercise using solfège and hand signs or numbers. Each measure uses tones from the F major or D minor chords. Can you tell which? Sing this exercise in a two-part round, one measure apart.

la   do   mi   do   mi   so   mi
6   1   3   1   3   5   3

Singing: "Welcome Now in Peace"

Do you know any words that mean more than one thing? The Hebrew word "shalom" means hello, welcome, farewell, and peace. When you meet a friend or leave a friend, you can use "shalom" as a greeting or a farewell.

Read the text of "Welcome Now in Peace." Discuss the pronunciation of the Hebrew words.

Now turn to the music for "Welcome Now in Peace" on page 32.

HOW DID YOU DO?

Just as you weave friendships, your voices wove together in greetings and wishes for peace. Think about your preparation and performance of "Welcome Now in Peace."
1. Explain how you know if a piece is in D minor or F major. What is the same? What is different? How well can you sight-sing in D minor?
2. Can you hear the difference between major and minor chords? Listen to some chords and signal, pointing your thumb up for major and down for minor, whether they are major or minor.

3. Listen to a small ensemble sing this piece. Describe the criteria you will use to evaluate whether the performance was well done. What will you listen for? What will you look for?
4. Write an assessment of your performance of "Welcome Now in Peace." Tell what you have learned, what you do well, what needs work, and how you feel about your performance of this piece.

Composed for the Tacoma Youth Chorus, Tacoma, Washington

Welcome Now in Peace

Hevenu Shalom A'leychem

Israeli Folksong
Vocal Arr. Judith Herrington
Accompaniment Sara Glick

Two-part, Accompanied

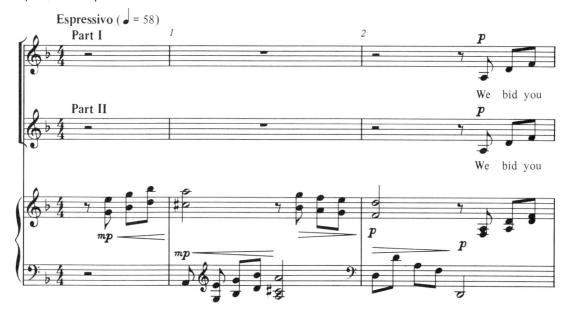

Reprinted by permission.

*Omit lower 3rd of R. H. if desired.

*optional meno mosso (♩ = 58) with
poco a poco accel. at measure 45

Silent the Forests

COMPOSER: *Eugene Butler*
TEXT: *Torquato Tasso (1544-1595)*

CHORAL MUSIC TERMS

altered tones

chromatic

flat (♭)

half steps

natural (♮)

sharp (♯)

VOICING

SSA

PERFORMANCE STYLE

Slowly

Accompanied by piano

FOCUS

- Sing softly with control.
- Identify half steps and altered tones.
- Sing descending chromatic passages.

Warming Up

Vocal Warm-Up 1

Practice your breathing. Place your hands on your waist with your elbows pointed outward. Now bark like a) a Pekingese, b) a fox terrier, and c) a Great Dane. Describe the difference in each sound. Did you notice your hands moving at your waist as your diaphragm supported the sound?

Vocal Warm-Up 2

Sing this exercise using staccato articulation, supported from the diaphragm. Can you sing it softly, and still use support and control? Move up by a half step on each repeat.

Sight-Singing 1

Read and sing each of these exercises alone using solfège and hand signs or numbers, then divide into four groups and sing them together.

Sight-Singing 2

First look at the alto line, and notice the altered tones and descending chromatic line. Sing *si* for D♯ and *fi* for C♯. First, all sight-sing each part separately. Then divide into three voice parts and sing them together. Tune each pitch carefully before moving on.

Singing: "Silent the Forests"

Think of the difference between quiet and silent. Is a forest ever silent? Is the sea ever waveless? Are winds ever completely at peace? When are words quiet? When are they silent?

Read the text of "Silent the Forests." What is the author trying to say?

Now turn to the music for "Silent the Forests" on page 40.

HOW DID YOU DO?

When you sing softly, there is a mystery that helps convey quiet—even silent—thoughts. Think about your preparation and performance of "Silent the Forests."
1. Describe how you control your breath when you sing softly. Sing your line from measures 3–6 in "Silent the Forests" to demonstrate.
2. Explain what it means if a tone is "altered." Point to some altered tones in "Silent the Forests."
3. Tell what a sharp, a flat, and a natural do to a note.
4. Define a chromatic passage. Sing the line with the chromatic passage in the Sight-Singing 2 exercise.
5. Do you think the music enhances the text of "Silent the Forests"? Why or why not? Be specific about your reasons, and give examples.

Silent the Forests

Eugene Butler
Torquato Tasso

SSA Women's Voices Accompanied

My Beloved

COMPOSER: *Johannes Brahms* (1833–1897)
ENGLISH TEXT: *Douglas McEwen*
EDITED BY: *Douglas McEwen*

CHORAL MUSIC TERMS

form

peak

phrase

section

3/4 meter

VOICING

Two-part chorus

PERFORMANCE STYLE

Slow

Accompanied by piano

FOCUS

- Read and sing in 3/4 meter.
- Identify parts of a phrase.
- Shape phrases correctly while singing.
- Identify sections and form of a piece.

Warming Up

Vocal Warm-Up

Sing this exercise using solfège and hand signs or numbers. Move up or down a half step as you repeat. Clearly articulate the dotted rhythm in the first measure. Notice the 3/4 meter. The 3 tells you there are 3 beats in a measure, and the 4 tells you that a quarter note gets one beat.

Sight-Singing

First, read this exercise with your eyes. Notice the musical features—the key and meter signatures, same and different sections, and steps and skips. The breath marks show phrases. Where is the peak of each phrase? You will need to build energy toward the peak, then release to the end of the phrase. Now sight-sing using solfège and hand signs or numbers.

Singing: "My Beloved"

Music's structure can be compared to our spoken language. Can you tell the meaning of the word *phrase* in language?

A musical phrase is a musical thought, containing a beginning, peak, and end. It is like a phrase in language. Musical phrases are combined into sentences. The sentences are grouped into sections, which loosely resemble paragraphs.

Now turn to the music for "My Beloved" on page 45.

HOW DID YOU DO?

?
?
?

Shaping phrases helps communicate the meaning of both music and text. Think about your preparation and performance of "My Beloved."

1. Describe 3/4 meter by telling what each number means. Now sing the Sight-Singing exercise to show that you can feel and sing 3/4 meter.

2. How do you shape a phrase? Sing the first phrase of "My Beloved" to demonstrate your skill.

3. What is the form of "My Beloved"? How do you know? What clues are in the music? Does form have anything to do with phrases?

4. Make a tape recording of your ensemble's performance of "My Beloved." After listening to a playback, describe and critique in writing how well the ensemble performed phrases. Make a recommendation to the group about what they should continue doing and what they could improve.

My Beloved

#13 from "Neue Liebeslieder"

(New Love songs)

Johannes Brahms, op. 65
Edited by Douglas McEwen
English text by Douglas McEwen

Two-part Chorus of Women's Voices
with Piano Four-hand Accompaniment

Fresh Is the Maytime

COMPOSER: *Johann Hermann Schein (1586–1630)*

EDITED BY: *Don Malin*

CHORAL MUSIC TERMS

bright vocal tone quality

chords

harmony

part independence

VOICING

SSA

PERFORMANCE STYLE

Joyful

A cappella

FOCUS

- Sing with a bright vocal tone quality.
- Sing a part independently with two other parts.
- Sing with correct German pronunciation.

Warming Up

Vocal Warm-Up

Sing this exercise using first *loo*, then *nee*. Which syllable allows you to get the tone high in your head? Work for a light, bright vocal tone quality. Move up by a half step on each repeat.

Loo loo loo loo loo.
Nee

Sight-Singing

Notice that the tonal center is G, or *so*. This gives the piece a modal feeling, typical of Renaissance music. First, all sight-sing each part separately, then divide into two voice parts and sing them together. Listen to both voice parts and tune the harmonies as you sing.

Singing: "Fresh Is the Maytime"

A painter can decide to use bright or dark colors to convey a mood or style. As a singer, you can choose bright or dark vowels, depending upon the piece you sing. Sing these tones, using the vowels indicated:

mee   meh   moh   moo

Which sound is bright? Which sound is dark? What mouth position causes each. Find the vowels in measures 1–12 of "Fresh Is the Maytime" on page 52. Brighten vowels by using the *ee* or *ih* mouth position.

Now sing the music for "Fresh Is the Maytime."

HOW DID YOU DO?

?
?
?
?

In the seventeenth century, the month of May was a time to be joyful, celebrating the end of winter and the beginning of spring. Think about your preparation and performance of "Fresh Is the Maytime."
1. How did you learn to create a bright vocal tone color? Demonstrate by singing measures 1–12 of your voice part to "Fresh Is the Maytime."
2. How well can you sing your part independently when other parts are being sung? Choose a section of "Fresh Is the Maytime" and sing it with two classmates, showing your skill at holding your own voice part while others sing theirs.

3. How is your German pronunciation? Speak measures 1–12 in rhythm to show your skill.
4. Write a critique of your learning and performance in this lesson. Assess your vocal tone color, part independence, and German pronunciation. Tell what you have learned, how you have improved, and what you need to work on.
5. State whether you think your ensemble's performance evoked feelings or emotions in the audience. Were they the feelings and emotions the composer intended? How do you know?

Fresh Is the Maytime

Der Kühle Maien

Johann Hermann Schein (1586–1630)
Edited by Don Malin
English Translation by Don Malin

SSA, Unaccompanied

Dame Night-in - gale's Sweet song pre - vails Re - sound - ing through green-wood fair.
Frau Nach-ti - gall lässt ih - ren Schall im grü - nen Wald an - hö - ren.

Dame Night-in - gale's Sweet song pre - vails Re - sound - ing through green-wood fair.
Frau Nach-ti - gall lässt ih - ren Schall im grü - nen Wald an - hö - ren.

Dame Night-in - gale's Sweet song pre - vails Re - sound - ing through green-wood fair.
Frau Nach-ti - gall lässt ih - ren Schall im grü - nen Wald an - hö - ren.

Birds all re - joice As with one voice Wood mu - sic is ev - 'ry - where.
All Vö - ge - lein mit stim - men ein, die Wald - mu-sik ver - meh - ren.

Birds all re - joice As with one voice Wood mu - sic is ev - 'ry - where.
All Vö - ge - lein mit stim - men ein, die Wald - mu-sik ver - meh - ren.

Birds all re - joice As with one voice Wood mu - sic is ev - 'ry - where.
All Vö - ge - lein mit stim - men ein, die Wald - mu-sik ver - meh - ren.

LESSON 9

Who Has Seen the Wind?

CHORAL MUSIC TERMS

changing meter

meter

rhythm

sizzle rhythms

strophic form

stony beat

COMPOSER: *Robert E. Kreutz*
TEXT: *Christina Rossetti* (1830–1894)

VOICING
SA

PERFORMANCE STYLE
With quiet flow
Accompanied by piano

FOCUS
- Read and sizzle rhythms in changing meters.
- Identify characteristics and sing in strophic form.

Warming Up

Rhythm Drill

Read and "sizzle" this rhythm, using a *tsss* sound. Be very accurate, and sustain the long tones for their full value. Have a classmate tap the steady beat audibly as you read.

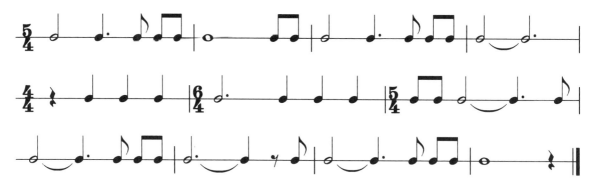

Vocal Warm-Up

Sing this Warm-Up using solfège and hand signs or numbers. Tune each interval accurately as you sing. Notice the steps, skips, and leaps as the intervals get farther apart.

Sight-Singing

Clap the rhythm of each line of this exercise as a classmate taps the steady beat. Keep the quarter note constant, noticing the different meters. Now sight-sing the exercise using solfège and hand signs or numbers.

Singing: "Who Has Seen the Wind?"

Beats can be grouped in many ways, but you are probably used to groups of two, three, or four beats in a measure. Walk the beat, and clap the strong beat (beat 1) for sets of two, then three, then four. When your group beats in fives, they are usually felt as 2+3 or 3+2. When you walk, count to five, but clap on beats 1 and 3. Start again and clap on beats 1 and 4.

Now you are ready to read a piece with beats in sets of three, four, five, and six. See if you can figure out why the composer would shift meters like this!

Now turn to the music for "Who Has Seen the Wind?" on page 58.

HOW DID YOU DO?

Were you steady enough to withstand the shifting meters? Think about your preparation and performance of "Who Has Seen the Wind?"

1. How well can you read rhythms when the meter keeps changing? Demonstrate by "sizzling" measures 3–13 of "Who Has Seen the Wind?"

2. Describe the characteristics of strophic form. Is "Who Has Seen the Wind?" strophic? Give specific examples that match the description.

3. If you were evaluating an ensemble singing "Who Has Seen the Wind?" what criteria would you use to determine whether or not it was a good performance? How would you assess your ensemble's performance?

Who Has Seen the Wind?

Robert E. Kreutz
Christina Rossetti

SA, Accompanied

I Never Saw a Moor

COMPOSER: *Michael Larkin*
TEXT: *Emily Dickinson* (1830-1886)

CHORAL MUSIC TERMS

major tonality

melodic leaps

mood

musical characteristics

stepwise melodic motion

VOICING

SSA

PERFORMANCE STYLE

Moderately, flowing
Accompanied by keyboard

FOCUS

- Identify and sight-sing stepwise melodies.
- Sight-sing in major tonality.
- Identify musical characteristics that enhance the mood of a poem.

Warming Up

Vocal Warm-Up

Sing this warm-up using the syllables provided. Bend forward at the waist as you sing up the scale, and return to upright position as you descend the scale. Give good, full resonance to the "m" of each syllable, and keep the tone focused in the mask of the face. Keep your mouth rounded to avoid spreading the vowel sounds. Move up by half steps on each repeat.

Sight-Singing

Sight-sing all three parts together in ensemble, using solfège and hand signs or numbers. Listen carefully as you tune to the other voice lines, comparing their rhythmic movement to yours. Can you read this straight through the first time? Where are the steps and leaps in your voice part?

Singing: "I Never Saw a Moor"

If you watch a child stepping and leaping, you will notice that the steps are much more in control, but the leaps are far more exciting. Your voice can move in steps and leaps with the same effect. Sing a scale up and down using solfège and hand signs or numbers. Sing the tonic chord up and down (*do, mi, so, do¹, so, mi,* and *do*). With half the ensemble singing the scale, the others will sing the triad. Then switch roles.

Now turn to the music for "I Never Saw a Moor" on page 66.

HOW DID YOU DO? ? ? ?

Step by step, you have learned the concepts and skills necessary to sing "I Never Saw a Moor." Think about your preparation and performance of "I Never Saw a Moor."

1. Define the musical characteristics of a stepwise melody, and how you recognize it in notation.

2. Sing a major scale up and down to show your understanding of major tonality.

3. Describe the stepwise melodic movement in your voice line of "I Never Saw a Moor."

4. Decide what three performance characteristics are most important to this piece. What would be a satisfactory, good, or excellent performance for each of these characteristics? Make a tape of your ensemble's performance. Listen to a playback; then rate each of these characteristics according to your list.

I Never Saw a Moor

Music by Michael Larkin
Text by Emily Dickinson

SSA, Accompanied

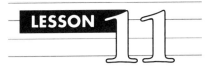

Arruru

Spanish Carol

ARRANGERS: *Ruth E. Dwyer and Thomas Gerber*

CHORAL MUSIC TERMS

harmony

legato articulation

staccato articulation

thirds

VOICING

Two-part chorus

PERFORMANCE STYLE

Rocking
Accompanied by piano

FOCUS

* Sing a harmony part in thirds.
* Use staccato and legato articulation.
* Identify some characteristics of Spanish music.

Warming Up

Vocal Warm-Up

Sing this warm-up using the word "Arruru." Sing the first measure legato, and the second measure staccato. Use your diaphragm to perform the staccato articulation. Sway as you sing, and roll the "r"s. Move up by half steps on each repetition.

Ah - roo - roo, roo-hoo-hoo-hoo - hoo.

Sight-Singing

Sight-sing this exercise twice using solfège and hand signs or numbers, switching parts the second time through. Notice the harmony in thirds, a common harmonization in Spanish folk music.

Singing: "Arruru"

You have probably heard Spanish folk music at some time, and remember what it sounds like. Describe some of the musical characteristics that you imagine when you think of Spanish folk music.

One characteristic of Spanish folk music is that the accompaniment is often performed on a guitar. Look through the notation of the accompaniment to find places where the piano might be imitating the sound of a guitar.

Now turn to the music for "Arruru" on page 73.

HOW DID YOU DO?

? ?

Spanish folk music has a highly distinctive style. Think about your preparation and performance of "Arruru."
1. Can you sing harmony in thirds? Sing measures 8–11 of "Arruru" with a classmate to demonstrate your skill.
2. Describe the difference between staccato and legato articulation, and tell how you used these in "Arruru."

3. Listen to a tape of your ensemble's performance of "Arruru" and discuss the characteristics of Spanish folk music that are present in this song.

Arruru

Spanish Carol
Arranged by Ruth E. Dwyer and
Thomas Gerber

Two-part Chorus with Piano

1. Se - ño - ra do - ña Ma -
2. The shep-herds are slow - ly

ri - a,_____ I bring you my lit - tle one, Se -
wind - ing_____ their way from the dis - tant hills. The

one. He'll help you to rock the cra - dle,_____ Where-
hills. To wit - ness the new-born ba - by_____ they've

in lies your new- born son.
braved all of win- ter's ills.
A - rru - ru,
A - rru - ru,
Duer-

me- te, Ni - ño Je - sús.
A - rru - sús.

To Coda ⊕ (last time)

D.S. 𝄋 al Coda
with repeats

Coda
⊕

a piacere
pp
subito
cresc.

blaze in the win-try sky, the dia-mond of Beth-le -

1. hem, A - hem.

2. How

LESSON 12

Peace Today Descends from Heaven

CHORAL MUSIC TERMS

imitative

melismatic

syllabic

3/2 meter

2/2 meter

COMPOSER: *Alessandro Grandi (c. 1575–1630)*
TRANSLATED AND EDITED BY: Dr. William Tortolano

VOICING

SA

PERFORMANCE STYLE

Slowly
Accompanied by keyboard

FOCUS

• Read and perform in 2/2 and 3/2 meter.
• Identify and perform syllabic, melismatic, and imitative passages.

Warming Up

Rhythm Drill

Clap these rhythms as someone taps the half-note pulse throughout. Notice the shift from beats in sets of two to beats in sets of three, and stress the strong beat at the beginning of each measure. What visual clue tells you to expect imitative style?

Vocal Warm-Up

Sing this exercise using a sigh, maintaining good breath support.

Sight-Singing

Clap the rhythm first, then sight-sing this exercise using solfège and hand signs or numbers. Watch for the changing meter as you read.

Singing: "Peace Today Descends from Heaven"

A composer can use text in many ways. Read this text out loud:

Now, today, peace descends from heaven. Alleluia!

Be a composer for the text in these ways:

- Sing one pitch for each syllable of the text.
- Sing each syllable for more than one pitch, stretching it out into a long thread. (When you do this, you create a *melismatic passage.*)
- With a partner, read the text with the same rhythm, but different pitches that create harmony.
- Next, wait while your partner imitates each word or group of words that you sing, before you go on.

Can you tell which of these is syllabic, melismatic, and imitative?

Now turn to the music for "Peace Today Descends from Heaven" on page 79.

HOW DID YOU DO?

? ? ?

You needed to use known information in new ways to learn this piece. Think about your preparation and performance of "Peace Today Descends from Heaven."

1. Tell how 2/2 and 3/2 meter work, then clap the Rhythm Drill, or sing the Sight-Singing exercise in a duet to show your skill.

2. Describe the difference between syllabic, melismatic, and imitative treatment of text. As you sing "Peace Today Descends from Heaven," signal by holding up one finger for syllabic, two fingers for melismatic and three fingers for imitative passages.

3. Compare "Peace Today Descends from Heaven" to other pieces you have sung in this book. How is it musically the same? How is it musically different?

4. Which characteristics of this piece do you prefer, and which would you change? List the factors you think led the composer to write the music as he did. (Consider cultural, historical, musical, and/or textual factors.)

Peace Today Descends from Heaven

Hodie, nobis de caelo

Alessandro Grandi
Translated and Edited by
Dr. William Tortolano

SA, Accompanied

day,   for all the earth cre - a - - - ted.   the *mel-*
e,   *per to - tum mun -dum, per to - tum mun - - dum*

sweet - ness of our peace and joy,   joy ——————— is made known to
li - flu-i, mel - li - flu-i,   *fac - - - - ti sunt mi -*

us.   Al-le-lu - ia,   Al-le-lu - ia,   Al - le - lu - -
hi.

Al-le-lu-ia,   Al-le-lu-ia,

ia, Al-le-lu - ia, Al - - le - lu - ia,

Al-le-lu - ia, Al - le - - - lu - ia,

Al - le - - - - lu - ia, Al - le - lu-

Al - le - - - - lu - ia, Al - le - lu -

da, Al - - le - lu - ia.

ia, Al - - le - lu - ia.

Peace Today Descends from Heaven **85**

LESSON 13

Os Justi

COMPOSER: *Eleanor Daley*
TEXT: *Psalm 37:30–31*

CHORAL MUSIC TERMS

consonants

dark tone quality

diction

vowels

VOICING

SSAA

PERFORMANCE STYLE

Slowly in two

A cappella

FOCUS

• Sing with a dark tone quality.

• Sing with correct diction.

Warming Up

Vocal Warm-Up

Sigh as though you have finished a difficult chore. Then start high and begin sighing downward, making an upward motion with your hands. Now use the same sighing breath to sing this Warm-Up. Move up or down by half steps on each repeat.

Sight-Singing

Sight-sing each part separately, using solfège and hand signs or numbers. Now sing both parts together. Switch parts. Sing this exercise using first a light tone quality, then a darker one.

Singing: "Os Justi"

A performer can choose tone quality to match the mood and message of a composition. Sing:

"The mouth of the righteous speaketh wisdom"

on one pitch. First form a round mouth, and sing the words, focusing on the vowels. Next, form a round mouth, then drop the jaw as much as possible as you sing.

Describe the difference between these two tone qualities, and when each would be appropriate to use.

Now turn to the music for "Os Justi" on page 88.

HOW DID YOU DO?

?

The composer writes the piece, but the performer interprets it, deciding how to bring the message to the audience. Think about your preparation and performance of "Os Justi."

1. Describe how to create a dark tone quality as you sing, then sing from the beginning of "Os Justi" to A, demonstrating this tone quality.

2. Tell a neighbor what you need to think about to have good diction, demonstrating with examples from "Os Justi."

3. Write a "diction manual" for an imaginary newcomer to your ensemble, informing them what is expected to create good diction.

To El's Angels

Os Justi

Eleanor Daley
Psalm 37:30–31

SSAA, A cappella

Translation: The mouth of the righteous speaketh wisdom, and his tongue talketh of judgement.
The law of God is in his heart; none of his steps shall slide. (Psalm 37:30-31)

LESSON 14

Dance on My Heart

COMPOSER: *Allen Koepke*
TEXT: *Allen Koepke*

CHORAL MUSIC TERMS

key signatures

mixed meter

rhythm

syncopated rhythms

VOICING

SSA

PERFORMANCE STYLE

Sprightly
Accompanied by piano

FOCUS

- Read rhythms in mixed meter.
- Identify and perform syncopated rhythms.
- Read and sing in two keys.

Warming Up

Rhythm Drill

Read and clap this rhythm over a steady eighth-note pulse. You will not need the pulse until you get to the 7/8 measure—then you will be glad it is there! Point out the syncopated rhythms.

Vocal Warm-Up

Sing this exercise using solfège and hand signs or numbers. Move up or down by half steps on the repeats. Now sing the exercise to practice forming vowels correctly, using *mah, meh, mee, moh,* and *moo.*

Sight-Singing

First, speak and clap the rhythms. Then sight-sing both exercises slowly, tuning each chord. Sing them more and more quickly, keeping the tuning accurate. How are these two exercises different?

 Singing: "Dance on My Heart"

A musical score is like a map. It won't help you much until you know how to read it. Look at "Dance on My Heart." Read the text, following the directions very carefully. Can you find your way through this word map without getting lost?

Tell the story in your own words, verse by verse.

Now turn to the music for "Dance on My Heart" on page 92.

HOW DID YOU DO?

?
?

By now, even a complicated map shouldn't stop you from singing from the heart. Think about your preparation and performance of "Dance on My Heart."
1. Tell how you negotiate changing from 4/4 to 7/8 meter, then clap the Rhythm Drill to show your skill.
2. Describe how syncopated rhythms work, then point some out in the notation of "Dance on My Heart."

3. Tell which two keys are used in "Dance on My Heart." How are they the same? How are they different? Sing the two Sight-Singing exercises to show your ability to sing in these two keys.
4. Write an imaginary radio critique of your ensemble's performance of "Dance on My Heart," comparing it to similar or exemplary models. Record the report, with yourself as the reporter for a local radio station.

Dance on My Heart

Allen Koepke

SSA, Accompanied

I'm a- dor - ing - ly sweet." (to m. 11, v. 2)
you'll___ be sat - is - fied." (to m. 20-21, v. 3)
say___ you'll be my wife." (to m. 20-21, v. 5)

3. "Well" she re - plied, "I'd make my se - lec - tion, and you'd re - ceive my
5. "Sir," she re - plied, "you are my se - lec - tion, and you'll re - ceive my

love and af - fec - tion if you danced on my heart,
love and af - fec - tion for you dance on my heart,

if you sang to my soul. But a - las, my heart is not
and you sing to my (v. 5 to coda m. 37)

pound-ing, and your songs are not sound-ing. There fore, I

can - not mar - ry you."

N.B.

DS al ⊕

(to m. 3, v.4.)

DS al ⊕

DS al ⊕

soul. I'll__ take__ your__ hand, wear your wed-ding__ band____

Yes, kind sir,____ I will mar-ry you!"____

Making Historical Connections

The Adoration of the Magi by Sandro Botticelli (1445–1510) reflects the Renaissance interest in religious subjects. Framing the central figures within the strong geometric pillars emphasized those subjects over others. Similar organizational principles are apparent in the Renaissance composers' ability to create intricate polyphonic works.

c. 1481. Sandro Botticelli. *The Adoration of the Magi.* (Detail.) Tempera on wood. 70 x 104 cm (27⅝ x 41″). National Gallery of Art, Washington, D.C. Andrew W. Mellon Collection.

Renaissance Period

c. 1430–1600

COMPOSERS

John Dunstable (c. 1390–1453)
Guillaume Dufay (1400–1474)
Josquin Desprez (c. 1440–1521)
Heinrich Isaac (c. 1450–1517)
Clement Janequin (c. 1485–1560)
Adrian Willaert (1490–1562)
Christopher Tye (c. 1500–c. 1572)
Thomas Tallis (1505–1585)
Andrea Gabrieli (1520–1586)
Giovanni Pierluigi da Palestrina (c. 1525–1594)
Orlande de Lassus (1532–1594)
William Byrd (1543–1623)
Thomas Morley (c. 1557–c. 1602)
Michael Praetorius (c. 1571–1621)
Thomas Weelkes (1575–1623)

ARTISTS

Donatello (1386–1466)
Sandro Botticelli (1445–1510)
Leonardo da Vinci (1452–1519)
Albrecht Dürer (1471–1528)
Michelangelo (1475–1564)
Raphael (1483–1520)
Titian (c. 1488–1576)

AUTHORS

Sir Thomas More (1478–1536)
Martin Luther (1483–1546)
Miguel de Cervantes (1547–1616)
Sir Walter Raleigh (c. 1552–1618)
Sir Philip Sidney (1554–1586)
William Shakespeare (1564–1616)

After completing this lesson, you will be able to:

- *Describe some of the major developments of the Renaissance period.*
- *Explain the difference between sacred music and secular music.*
- *Discuss the major musical forms of the Renaissance period.*
- *Identify at least three major composers of the Renaissance period.*

In the history of Western Europe, the period from around 1430 until 1600 is called the Renaissance. This name comes from a French word meaning "rebirth," and the period was in many ways a time of rebirth or renewal. The scholars and artists of the Renaissance made a conscious effort to reestablish the standards of intellectual and cultural greatness they saw in the accomplishments of the ancient Greeks and Romans. Although the great figures of the Renaissance may have been looking back to earlier cultures, they were not moving back; instead, they were moving radically ahead into modern times.

A Time of Discovery

The Renaissance was a time of discovery in many fields. Modern science and scientific methods began to develop. Scholars no longer simply accepted what they read. Rather, they realized that careful observation and experimentation could help them draw new conclusions about the world around them. The results of this approach were a series of important advancements in science, mathematics, and technology. Better clocks and navigating instruments became available; scientists began to develop better lenses for instruments such as telescopes and microscopes. Astronomers established that the Earth and other planets revolved around the sun, and the positions of many stars were accurately calculated.

In part because of the technological advances of the period, the Renaissance was an era of increasing exploration and trade. For the first time, European sailing ships reached the southern coast of Africa, the Americas, and India. In 1519, the first successful round-the-world voyage was undertaken. These journeys brought a new, expanding sense of the world and an influx of new ideas—as well as new opportunities for trade—to the people of Renaissance Europe.

One technological advancement of the Renaissance had an impact on many aspects of life: the invention of the printing press with movable type, usually credited to Johann Gutenberg. Until this development, books had been copied by hand. The development of the printing press meant that books could be produced much more quickly and easily, and much less expensively. More and more people had access to books and the ideas they communicated, and thus prepared themselves to take advantage of this opportunity by learning to read both words and music. Books—of facts, of new ideas, and of music—were no longer the property of only the privileged.

CHORAL MUSIC TERMS

a cappella
Gregorian chant
madrigal
mass
motet
polyphony
sacred music
secular music

Gutenberg press; beginning of modern printing   Copenhagen becomes Danish capital   First printed music appears

c. 1435   **1445**   **1465**

1441   **1453**

Eton College and King's College,   Ottoman Turks capture Constantinople, marking end
Cambridge, founded   of Byzantine Empire

During the Renaissance, the Catholic church gradually lost some of the influence it had exerted as a center of learning, a formidable political power, and an important force in the daily lives of nearly all Europeans. Rejecting the absolute laws set down by the Church, though not necessarily rejecting any faith in God, Renaissance scholars accepted humanism, a belief in the dignity and value of individual human beings. In addition, the first Protestant churches were established, in opposition to the rule of the Catholic hierarchy.

A Renaissance of the Visual Arts

The developments and discoveries of the Renaissance were reflected in the arts of the period. The works of painters and sculptors became more lifelike and realistic. Painters gave new depth to their work by using perspective and by manipulating light and shadow; they also began using oil paints, which allowed them to revise and refine their work. Sculptors created more individualized human figures, and sculpture began to be considered a true art, rather than a craft.

Many paintings and sculptures of the Renaissance depicted religious subjects, especially scenes from the Bible. However, artists increasingly crafted works with non-religious subjects, often taken from Greek and Roman mythology.

Careful observation and an intense interest in the natural world helped Renaissance artists develop more realistic and individualized paintings and sculptures. Some of the most notable artists worked in several media and delved deeply into science as well. Leonardo da Vinci, one of the foremost painters and sculptors of the Renaissance, was also an architect, a scientist, an engineer, and a musician.

The Influence of the Catholic Church on Music

In the centuries preceding the Renaissance—a time usually called the Middle Ages—most composed music was for the Catholic church and performed as part of religious services. The most important musical form of the period was the **Gregorian chant,** *a melody sung in unison by male voices.* The chants were sung **a cappella**, *without instrumental accompaniment.* All the chants were composed in Latin, the language of all Church services at that time, and were based on sacred texts, often from the Book of Psalms in the Old Testament.

Although the earliest Gregorian chants consisted of a single melodic line, a second melodic line was added to most chants during the Middle Ages. This was the beginning of **polyphony**, *the simultaneous performance of two or more melodic lines.* In polyphonic music, each part begins at a different place, and each part is independent and important. The use of various kinds of polyphony has continued through the centuries; in fact, polyphony is a significant feature in some modern jazz compositions.

da Vinci sketches an early helicopter design

1483

Columbus lands in West Indies/Americas

1492

1473–1480

Sistine Chapel built

1488

Diaz sails around the Cape of Good Hope

1498

da Gama sails around Africa
and lands in India

The artists and architects of the Renaissance rediscovered Classical antiquity and were inspired by what they found. In 1547, Michelangelo (1475–1564) became chief architect for the replacement of the original basilica of Old St. Peter's. Architect Giacomo della Porta finished the dome 26 years after Michelangelo's death.

1546–64. Michelangelo. Exterior view, St. Peter's. St. Peter's Basilica, Vatican State, Rome, Italy. (Dome completed by Giacomo della Porta, 1590.)

Sacred Music of the Renaissance

During the Renaissance, the Catholic church continued to exert a strong influence on daily life and on the arts. Much of the important music composed during the Renaissance was **sacred music**, *music used in religious services.*

The two most important forms of sacred Renaissance music were the **mass**—*a long musical composition that includes the five major sections of the Catholic worship service*—and the **motet**—*a shorter choral work, set to Latin texts and used in religious services, but not part of the regular mass.* In the early years of the Renaissance, one of the most influential composers

1508   **1519**   Cortez conquers Mexico   **1529**   **1545**

1517   **1531**

Protestant Reformation begins in Germany with Luther's 95 Theses

Henry VIII declared head of the Church of England

1519

Magellan begins voyage around the world

of both masses and motets was John Dunstable. Dunstable developed a new harmonic structure of polyphony; his music helped establish the Renaissance as the "golden age of polyphony."

Later in the period, Josquin Desprez began to change the sound of Renaissance choral music. He believed that music should be structured to make the words of the text understandable, and he also thought that all the voices in a choral setting could be equal in importance. Desprez is considered one of the founders of Renaissance music, because he introduced three new musical concepts:

1. Homophonic harmonies, produced by chords that support a melody;
2. Motive imitation, short repeating melodies between voice parts;
3. A more natural cadence, or sense of conclusion.

During the Renaissance, instruments were added to accompany and echo the voices used in sacred music. Adrian Willaert was one of the first composers to combine voices, pipe organs, and other instruments. He also began to use dynamics and was among the first to compose for two imitative voices.

The first music for Protestant religious services was written during this period. Here, sacred music was sung not in Latin but in the languages of the worshipers. One of the most important leaders of the Protestant Reformation, Martin Luther, wrote German hymns that are still sung in Protestant churches today.

The Evolution of Secular Music

Secular music, *any music that is not sacred*, changed in quality and quantity during the Renaissance period. Secular music became increasingly important as the center of musical activity began to shift from churches to castles and towns. Many court and town musicians traveled throughout Europe, so new styles and musical ideas spread relatively rapidly.

The **madrigal**, *a secular form of music written in several imitative parts*, became popular during the Renaissance. Madrigals were composed by such musicians as Clement Janequin, Heinrich Isaac, Thomas Tallis, William Byrd, Thomas Morley, and Thomas Weelkes, to be sung by everyday people. Whole collections of songs in the madrigal form were printed in part books. A family might purchase a set of part books (one for soprano, one for alto, and so on); then family members and friends would gather around these part books and sing.

Most madrigals were composed for three or more voices. Typically, a madrigal was based on a secular poem and incorporated the expression of strong emotions, usually about love. The polyphony within madrigals was often quite challenging, even though the songs were intended primarily for home entertainment. Europeans of the noble and emerging middle classes placed an increased importance on the education of the individual; reading music and singing were considered essential aspects of that education.

Elizabeth I crowned Queen of England
(died 1603)

1558

Portuguese colonize Angola
and found São Paulo

1574

William Shakespeare begins play writing

c. 1590

1564

First violins made by Andrea Amati

1584

Sir Walter Raleigh discovers Virginia

1599

Globe Theatre built in London

Check Your Understanding

Recall

1. What were the most important differences between the music of the Middle Ages and the music of the Renaissance?

2. What is a cappella music?

3. What is polyphony?

4. What is the difference between a mass and a motet?

5. What is the difference between sacred music and secular music?

6. How are motets and madrigals alike? How are they different?

Thinking It Through

1. The word *polyphony* comes from two roots: poly, meaning *many*, and phony, meaning *sounds*. Explain the relationship between these roots and polyphonic music.

2. If you listened to a piece of unidentified music, what clues could help you decide whether it was a Renaissance composition?

Listening to...
Renaissance Music

CHORAL SELECTION

Thomas Weelkes — "As Vesta Was Descending"

Thomas Weelkes (1575–1623), an organist and church composer, was one of England's best madrigalists. "As Vesta Was Descending" is found in a collection of madrigals called *The Triumphes of Oriana*, published in 1601. This is a six-voice madrigal that uses text painting.

In the song "As Vesta Was Descending," Vesta is portrayed as the Roman goddess of the hearth fire coming down the hill with her servants, "Diana's darlings." (Diana is the protector of servants.) At the same time, Oriana (Queen Elizabeth I) is climbing the hill with her shepherd followers. When Vesta's attendants see the Queen, they desert Vesta and hurry down the hill to join Oriana, whereupon everyone sings the Queen's praises.

INSTRUMENTAL SELECTION

Andrea Gabrieli — Ricercar in the Twelfth Mode

Andrea Gabrieli (1520–1586) was the organist at St. Mark's Cathedral in Venice, Italy, from 1564 until his death. He composed instrumental as well as sacred and secular vocal music.

A *ricercar* is a polyphonic instrumental composition that uses imitation. "In the Twelfth Mode" means that it is based on a scale corresponding to C major.

104 *Choral Connections Level 3 Treble Voices*

RENAISSANCE CONNECTIONS

Introducing...
"I Go Before, My Charmer"

Thomas Morley

Setting the Stage

"I Go Before, My Charmer" is a canzonet, a song written for group singing during the Renaissance period. This madrigal has been written for two equal voices, and its imitative yet independent lines, and light, buoyant tempo provide the character so typical of Renaissance secular music. The meter changes, which seem a bit difficult today, were quite familiar to the Renaissance singer and also were typical of the period's music.

Meeting the Composer
Thomas Morley (c. 1557–1602)

Thomas Morley, best known for his madrigals and canzonets, was born in Norwich, England, and later became the organist of Norwich Cathedral. In 1588, he received his Bachelor of Music Degree from Oxford and became the organist of St. Paul's Cathedral.

Morley was also a printer, holding a monopoly on all music publications under a patent granted to him by the English government in 1598. In addition to publishing his own works, he acted as editor, arranger, translator, and music publisher of music by other composers.

I Go Before, My Charmer

COMPOSER: *Thomas Morley (c. 1557–1602)*
TEXT: *Unknown Authorship*

CHORAL MUSIC TERMS

canzonets

4/4 meter

imitative style

independent singing

madrigals

mixed meter

3/2 meter

VOICING

Two-part voices

PERFORMANCE STYLE

Moderately

A cappella

FOCUS

- Sing one part independently with another part.
- Identify and sing in imitative style.
- Read and sing rhythms in mixed meter, with 4/4 and 3/2 meter.

Warming Up

Rhythm Drill

Speak and clap this rhythm in two parts. Notice the imitative style. Can you describe how you will feel the pulse as you change from 4/4 to 3/2 meter? What will be equal?

Vocal Warm-Up

Sing this warm-up using solfège and hand signs or numbers, then using vowels with a consonant in front (*mah, meh, mee, moh, moo*). On measure 1, bend at the waist and touch your toes. On measure 2, return gradually to an upright position. Repeat this movement each time these measures are repeated. Move up or down a half step as you repeat.

do re mi fa so
1 2 3 4 5

Sight-Singing

Before singing, study this exercise and determine the form. Which phrases are the same? Sight-sing using solfège and hand signs or numbers. Can you sing accurately the first time through? Conduct in 4/4 as you sing.

Singing: "I Go Before, My Charmer"

What entertainment can you imagine if there were no movies, television or radio, and not even electricity for light!

As printed secular music became easily accessible, many canzonets and madrigals were written for public use. The texts were light and charming, and often had a romantic theme. During the Renaissance, a popular form of entertainment was to invite guests for dinner and then sing around the table after supper.

Read the text of "I Go Before, My Charmer" starting on page 108. Then tell the story in your own words.

Now sing "I Go Before, My Charmer."

HOW DID YOU DO?

?
?
?

You have probably built skills and understanding by now and found you had no dilemma in performing "I Go Before, My Charmer" successfully. Think about your preparation and performance of "I Go Before, My Charmer."

1. How well can you sing your voice part alone? How well can you sing it when the other part is being sung? Is it easier with the full ensemble, or would it be easier in a smaller group?

2. Describe the characteristics of imitative style, and point out where it can be heard and seen in "I Go Before, My Charmer."

3. Tell how you felt the shift from 4/4 to 3/2 meter. What remains the same? Clap the rhythm drill to show your skill at making this change.

4. Assess your ensemble's performance of "I Go Before, My Charmer." What will your criteria for assessment be?

I Go Before, My Charmer

Thomas Morley (c. 1557–1602)
Text of unknown authorship
Edited by G. Wallace Woodworth

Canzonet for Unaccompanied Two-part Voices

Dal - ly dal - ly dal - ly dal - ly dal - ly dal - ly dal - ly dal -

dal - ly dal - ly dal - ly dal - ly dal - ly dal - ly dal -

pp legato
ly. There we will to - geth - er, Sweet - ly kiss each o - ther, And like two wan -

pp legato
ly. There we will to - geth - er, Sweet - ly kiss each o - ther, And like two wan -

pp legato

pp legato sempre
tons Dal - ly dal - ly dal - ly dal - ly dal - ly dal - ly,

pp legato sempre
tons Dal - ly dal - ly dal - ly dal - ly, Dal - ly

pp legato sempre *p*

rit.
Dal - ly dal - ly dal - ly dal - ly dal - ly dal - ly dal - ly.

rit.
dal - ly dal - ly dal - ly dal - ly dal - ly dal - ly dal - ly.

rit.

E. C. SCHIRMER • BOSTON | Music Publishers

▲ **Attention to detail, particularly in direct and reflected light in mirrors and doorways, characterizes this work of Diego Velázquez (1599–1660). The challenge to the viewer to find all the images in *Las Meninas* equals the challenge to comprehend the intricacies in a Bach fugue or concerto, representative musical works of the same period.**

1656. Diego Velázquez. *Las Meninas*. Oil on canvas. 3.20 x 2.76 m (10'5" x 9'). Museo del Prado, Madrid, Spain.

Baroque Period

COMPOSERS

Claudio Monteverdi (1567–1643)
Arcangelo Corelli (1643–1713)
Henry Purcell (1659–1695)
Antonio Vivaldi (1678–1741)
Georg Philipp Telemann (1681–1767)
Johann Sebastian Bach (1685–1750)
George Frideric Handel (1685–1759)

ARTISTS

El Greco (1541–1614)
Michelangelo da Caravaggio
(c.1565–1609)
Peter Paul Rubens (1577–1640)
Frans Hals (1580–1666)
Artemisia Gentileschi (1593–1653)
Gianlorenzo Bernini (1598–1680)
Diego Velazquez (1599–1660)
Rembrandt van Rijn (1606–1669)
Judith Leyser (1609–1660)

AUTHORS

John Donne (c.1573–1631)
Rene Descartes (1596–1650)
John Milton (1608–1674)
Molière (1622–1673)

After completing this lesson, you will be able to:

- Describe the general characteristics of Baroque visual arts.
- Discuss the most important differences between Renaissance music and Baroque music.
- Identify at least five new musical forms of the Baroque period.
- Identify at least four major composers of the Baroque period.

The artworks of the Renaissance reflect the ideas and ideals of the period. They are balanced and restrained; they communicate a sense of calm. The next period of European history—the Baroque period, which lasted from about 1600 until around 1750—was an age of reaction against the restraint and balance of the Renaissance. Baroque artists expressed the ideals of their own time by adding emotion, decoration, and opulence to their works.

A Time of Continued Development

The explorations and developments of the Renaissance continued into the Baroque period. European trade with distant lands increased, and European kingdoms sought to expand their power by establishing empires. The first European settlers left their homes and sailed to the Americas. People had a growing sense of possibility and excitement.

The study of science and mathematics continued to advance, and new technological developments were made. The basis of modern chemistry was established, and medical research, as well as medical practices, improved. The study of science became a more complex and consuming endeavor, one that no longer attracted the special interests of artists.

During the Baroque period, aristocrats—including emperors, kings, princes, and other nobles—seemed intent on displaying their wealth and power. Part of this display involved attracting great artists, including musicians, to their courts. Both the aristocracy and the Catholic church were generous patrons of the arts throughout the Baroque period. The artworks created during the Baroque period are typically large in scale and dramatic in effect. Painters and sculptors of the time built upon the forms established by Renaissance artists and added their own complex details and dramatic elaborations.

CHORAL MUSIC TERMS

arias

cantata

chorale

concerto grosso

continuo

movements

opera

oratorio

recitative

suite

Baroque Music

Baroque music reflected the same style exhibited in the visual arts of the time; it was written on a grand scale, full of vitality and emotion. Compositions typically had a strong sense of movement, often including a **continuo**, *a continually moving bass line.* Usually the melody was highly ornamental. In many compositions, additional ornamentations were improvised, or invented on the spur of the moment during performances.

Galileo
1564–1642

Henry Hudson explores
the Hudson River
1609

Pilgrims land in America
1620

Isaac Newton
1642–1727

Quakers arrive in Massachusetts
1656

1607
Jamestown, Virginia,
established settlement

1618–1648
Thirty Years' War

1636
Harvard College
founded

1643–1715
Reign of Louis XIV as King of France

1608
Telescope invented in Holland

During this period, instrumental music gained in importance, both in the church and as music commissioned for the entertainment of the courts of Europe. Vocal music also underwent changes. Instrumental accompaniments were increasingly added to both sacred and secular vocal works, and several new musical forms developed.

▲ **The ornate interior decor is reflected endlessly in the Hall of Mirrors, designed by François de Cuvilliés (1696–1768). Musical embellishment and ornamentation of the Baroque period provide similar stylistic elements in compositions by Johann Sebastian Bach and his contemporaries.**

1734–39. François de Cuvilliés. Hall of Mirrors, Amalienburg, Munich, Germany.

Instrumental Forms

As instrumental music grew more important, the musical instruments themselves were refined and their uses changed. The violin, previously a solo instrument, was added to ensemble groups. The harpsichord and the organ became the most important keyboard instruments.

Longer instrumental works were composed during the Baroque period. Often, these compositions consisted of several **movements**, *individual pieces that sound fairly complete within themselves but are part of a longer work.*

One of the new instrumental forms of the Baroque period was the **concerto grosso**. This *composition for a small chamber orchestra consists of several movements and features a moving bass line and an elaborate melody.* Most of the major Baroque composers wrote concerti grossi. Among the best known are *The Four Seasons* by Antonio Vivaldi and the set of six *Brandenburg Concertos* by Johann Sebastian Bach.

Another instrumental form that developed was the **suite**, *a set of musical movements, usually inspired by dances, of contrasting tempos and styles.* Suites and suite-related compositions were very popular during this time; the most famous suites were those composed by Bach.

Vocal and Mixed Forms

Vocal music became more varied and notably more dramatic during the Baroque period. Sacred music continued to be predominantly choral, but new instrumental accompaniment added greater variety and strength to many compositions. One of the new forms of the Baroque period was the **chorale**, or *hymn tune.* Chorales were

Johann Sebastian Bach

1685–1750

First American newspaper
established, *Boston News Letter*   Handel comes to England

1704   1710

1682   1685–1759   1706–1790

LaSalle explores   George Frideric Handel   Benjamin Franklin
the Mississippi

1687

Publication of Newton's *Mathematical Principles*

composed for Lutheran services, using German texts. They were easy to sing and to remember, so all members of a church congregation could join in.

A related Baroque form was the **cantata**, *a collection of compositions with instrumental accompaniment consisting of several movements based on related secular or sacred text segments.* The fact that this form could be composed as either a sacred or a secular work itself marks a new development of the period. Music directors at important Protestant churches were required to compose cantatas for weekly services. Bach, who served as a music director in Leipzig for 25 years, composed nearly 300 sacred cantatas.

Another mixed form from the Baroque period is the **oratorio**, *a composition for solo voices, chorus, and orchestra, that was an extended dramatic work on a literary or religious theme presented without theatrical action.* Like a cantata, an oratorio was composed to be performed in a concert setting, without costumes and scenery. However, the oratorio was written on a larger scale and told a story, usually religious, with plot and resolution. The oratorio was typically performed by a small chorus, an orchestra, and four vocal soloists.

Of all the new musical forms that developed during the Baroque period, perhaps the most characteristic is the **opera**, *a combination of singing, instrumental music, dancing, and drama that tells a story.* Opera combined many art forms, including drama, dance, architecture, and visual art, with music. And, in the true sense of Baroque style, opera was emotional and lavish. The best known composers of Baroque opera were Claudio Monteverdi, who wrote *Orfeo*, the first important opera, in 1607, and Henry Purcell.

The highlights of most operas are the **arias**, *dramatic songs for solo voices with orchestral accompaniment.* Another important feature of an opera is the **recitative**, *a vocal line that imitates the rhythm of speech.*

Check Your Understanding

Recall

1. What is a continuo?

2. What is a concerto grosso? Which Baroque composers are particularly remembered for this kind of composition?

3. What is a cantata?

4. What is the difference between an oratorio and an opera?

5. How are an aria and a recitative alike? How are they different?

6. List at least three adjectives you would use to describe the music of the Baroque period.

Thinking It Through

1. Identify one Baroque composition you have listened to. What characteristics mark that composition as a Baroque work?

2. For whom was Baroque music written? Who were the intended performers and the intended audience?

Listening to...

Baroque Music

CHORAL SELECTION

Bach — Cantata No. 140, Seventh Movement

The music of Johann Sebastian Bach (1685–1750) exemplifies the Baroque style of music. He was born at Eisenach, Germany, into a very musical family. He worked as a court organist and chamber musician to the Duke of Weimar. Bach fathered 20 children from two marriages, with four of his sons becoming well-known composers. Bach wrote roughly 295 cantatas as the music director of a Lutheran church One hundred ninety-five of these are still in existence today. Cantata No. 140 is one of Bach's most famous cantatas. The Seventh Movement brings back the chorale tune, set in a simple homophonic texture for four voices doubled by instruments.

INSTRUMENTAL SELECTION

Bach — Suite in No. 3 in D Major, Second Movement

The Baroque suite consists of a set of dance-inspired movements which are all in the same key and usually in two-part form, with the A and B sections repeated. Each movement has a different tempo, meter, and character, representing the music of different countries. The A section usually begins in the tonic key and modulates to the dominant, and the B section begins in the dominant key and returns to the tonic. Bach wrote four suites for orchestra. Suite No. 3 in D Major, "Air," is written for strings and continuo in the style of an Italian aria.

BAROQUE CONNECTIONS

Introducing...
"O Death, None Could Conquer Thee"

Johann Sebastian Bach

Setting the Stage

Some believe that Johann Sebastian Bach was the greatest composer that ever lived. The Baroque period ended with his death, yet the period lives on because of the legacy he left for all to study and enjoy today. Bach's influence can even be seen in contemporary music—especially jazz. The prominent feature of jazz is improvisation. Bach was the greatest of all improvisors. For example, take a close look at the left-hand bass line of the accompaniment in "O Death, None Could Conquer Thee." This is "notated improvisation" at its best: a typical walking bass line of the Baroque.

Take another look at this piece of music. Its typical Baroque style is exemplified in its steady tempo and stately setting. This would be a good song to use for improvising, if it were not for its sad text. However, just for fun try to improvise on the rhythm the way you will do in the warm-up exercise. Certainly Bach would approve!

Meeting the Composer
Johann Sebastian Bach (1685–1750)

Johann Sebastian Bach was born into a family that had produced musicians for several generations. However, his parents died when he was ten. Young Bach went to live with his brother, Johann Christoph, who gave him musical training. So thorough was his training that he became a masterful organist, and the output of music he composed staggers the imagination.

BAROQUE LESSON

O Death, None Could Conquer Thee

CHORAL MUSIC TERMS
enhancement of text

imitative style

independent singing

interweaving lines

minor key

COMPOSER: *Johann Sebastian Bach* (1685–1750)
ARRANGER: *Lee Kjelson*

VOICING
Two-part chorus

PERFORMANCE STYLE
Sustained

Accompanied by piano

FOCUS
- Read and sing in a minor key.
- Sing imitative and interweaving lines independently.
- Sing using correct German pronunciation.
- Identify musical enhancement of text.

Warming Up

Vocal Warm-Up
Sing this warm-up using solfège syllables or numbers. Move up or down a half step on each repeat.

Each time you sing the Warm-Up, try to spontaneously vary the rhythm, creating a rhythmic improvisation on the pitches. Keep the basic pitches the same, but add some imaginative rhythm. The example below will give you an idea, but once it is written down, it's no longer an improvisation.

Sight-Singing

Sight-sing this exercise in two parts. Notice how the lines weave together, using imitation and independent rhythms. Look for ways to get clues from the other voice part for your pitches after rests.

Singing: "O Death, None Could Conquer Thee"

What would you say to death? Read the text of "O Death, None Could Conquer Thee." What did the composer say to death? Why would such a text be chosen? What musical characteristics would you choose to set this text to if you were the composer? When might it be performed?

Now turn to the music for "O Death, None Could Conquer Thee" on page 120.

HOW DID YOU DO?

Even a mournful text can be hauntingly beautiful when well sung. Think about your preparation and performance of "O Death, None Could Conquer Thee."

1. Sing the Vocal Warm-up to show your ability to sing in a minor key.

2. Describe how the composer used imitative and interweaving lines in "O Death, None Could Conquer Thee." How well can you sing your part independently when the other part is being sung?

3. How well do you sing in German? What do you do well? What could be better?

4. How did Bach musically enhance the text of "O Death, None Could Conquer Thee?" What musical characteristics did he employ? Would you use the same ones if you were the composer? What would you do differently?

O Death, None Could Conquer Thee

(Den Tod, Niemand Zwingen Kunnt')

Two-part Chorus SA or TB (with Piano Accompaniment)

J. S. Bach
Arr. Lee R. Kjelson

c/o CPP/BELWIN, INC., Miami, Florida 33014

O Death, None Could Conquer Thee **123**

Anne Louis Girodet-Trioson (1767–1824), through this portrait of *Jean-Baptiste Bellay, Deputy of Santo Domingo,* expressed the interest of Europeans in revolution for the rights of the individual. As visual artists worked with such themes, composers were also influenced by similar revolutionary thought. The *Eroica Symphony in E-Flat* by Beethoven is one of many examples of music inspired by revolution.

1797. Anne Louis Girodet-Trioson. *Jean-Baptiste Bellay, Deputy of Santo Domingo.* (Detail.) Oil on canvas. 160 x 114 cm (63 x 45″). Musée National du Chateau de Versailles, Versailles, France.

Classical Period

1750–1820

After completing this lesson, you will be able to:

- Discuss the major changes that took place during the Classical period.
- Identify the ideals of the Classical arts.
- Discuss the most important musical forms of the Classical period.
- Identify the two most important Classical composers.

The emotion and drama of the Baroque period were followed by the clarity and simplicity of the Classical period. The word *Classical* has many meanings. It refers to the works and ideas of ancient Greece and Rome. It also refers to the period of European art and music that lasted from about 1750 until around 1820. During this time, artists "looked back" to the standards of balance and unity they saw in ancient Greek and Roman artworks.

The Age of Enlightenment

The Classical period is often called the Age of Enlightenment. It was a time when people put their faith in reason and thought, not in tradition and emotion. It was also a time of great faith in "progress." Members of the growing middle classes believed that their rights could and would be established and that the power and privilege of the aristocracy would be curtailed.

The attitudes of the Classical period were reflected in the major political events of the era. The American colonists revolted against their British rulers and established an independent United States. Thirteen years after the signing of the Declaration of Independence, the French Revolution began; this uprising established a new government and a new societal structure in France.

During the Classical period, the Catholic church's support of the arts declined sharply. However, noble and wealthy individuals and families commissioned artworks of all kinds in increasing numbers. In spite of this patronage, some important visual artists created works that poked subtle fun at the activities and attitudes of the aristocracy.

The paintings, sculpture, and architecture of this period are usually referred to as Neoclassical. (The prefix *neo-* adds the meaning "new"; this term distinguishes Neoclassical artworks from the Classical artworks created in ancient Greece and Rome.) Neoclassical works stress the balance and grandeur that artists saw in the ancient Classical works. Painters such as Jacques Louis David used ancient Roman settings and emphasized firm lines and clear structures. The simpler and grand styles developed in painting, sculpture, and architecture were both an evocation of Classical balance and a reaction against the emotional excesses of late Baroque art.

COMPOSERS

Franz Joseph Haydn (1732–1809)
Wolfgang Amadeus Mozart (1756–1791)
Luigi Cherubini (1760–1842)
Ludwig van Beethoven (1770–1827)
Vincento Bellini (1801–1835)

ARTISTS

Antoine Watteau (1684–1721)
Francois Boucher (1703–1770)
Jean-Honoré Fragonard (1732–1806)
Francisco Gôya (1746–1828)
Jacques Louis David (1748–1825)
Anne Louis Girodet-Trioson (1767–1824)

AUTHORS

Jonathan Swift (1667–1745)
Samuel Richardson (1689–1761)
Voltaire (1694–1778)
Henry Fielding (1707–1754)
Wolfgang Goethe (1749–1832)
Friedrich von Schiller (1759–1805)
Jane Austen (1775–1817)

CHORAL MUSIC TERMS
chamber music
sonata form
string quartets
symphony

Swift's *Gulliver's Travels* published

1726

George Washington

1732–1799

Thomas Jefferson

1743–1826

American Revolutionary War fought

1775–1783

1732–1757

Franklin writes *Poor Richard's Almanac*

1775

James Watt invents the steam engine

Music of the Classical Period

Like Neoclassical paintings, sculpture, and architecture, Classical music left behind the extreme drama and emotion of the Baroque period. Exaggerated embellishments and improvisations had no place in Classical compositions. Instead, Classical music emphasized precision and balance. An essential characteristic of the period was a careful balance between the content of the music and the form in which it was expressed.

During this period, middle-class people took an increasing interest in music. Composers responded by writing works that were accessible to the general public. Comic operas began to replace the serious operas of Baroque times. Dance music, including familiar folk tunes, were included in many compositions. Music, like other art forms, gradually became available to a wider range of the population.

Vocal and mixed forms, especially the opera and the oratorio, continued to develop during the Classical period. However, the most important Classical developments came in instrumental music, which gained in importance during this time.

Interest in archeology, particularly Greek and Roman models, resulted in the design of the library at Kenwood House by Robert Adam. This room combines Roman stucco ornamentation with the symmetry and geometric precision of the Classical period. Symmetry and precision are vital elements in musical compositions of the Classical period along with formal design and structure.

Begun in 1767. Robert Adam. Library at Kenwood House. London, England.

Chamber music—*music for a small group of instruments designed to be played in a room (or chamber) rather than in a public concert hall*—became significant during the Classical period. Such compositions are generally light and entertaining, both for the performers and for the listeners. The most popular Classical chamber music compositions were **string quartets**, *pieces composed for two violins, a viola, and a cello.*

Another important instrumental form of the Classical period was the **sonata form**, *a movement written in A A' B A form.* The sonata form begins with a theme (A), which is then repeated with elaboration (A'). Then comes a contrasting development (B), and the form closes with a return to the original theme (A).

The concerto also changed and developed during the Classical period. The Baroque concerto featured an instrumental group supported by an orchestra. The Classical concerto, by contrast, became a work for an instrumental soloist—often a pianist, but also a violinist, trumpeter, clarinetist, bassoonist, or cellist—and orchestra.

American Declaration of Independence signed

▼ 1776

Federal Government established in America

▼ 1789

▲ 1789

French Revolution begins

▲ 1808

Roman excavations begin at Pompeii, Italy

In a Classical concerto, the soloist and the orchestra are equals—another example of the Classical emphasis on balance.

Perhaps the most important instrumental development of the period was the **symphony**, *a large-scale piece for orchestra in three or more movements*. A Classical symphony usually consisted of four movements in this order: 1) A dramatic, fast movement; 2) A slow movement, often in sonata form; 3) A dance-style movement; 4) An exciting, fast movement.

Major Classical Composers

The Classical period was dominated by two composers, Franz Joseph Haydn and Wolfgang Amadeus Mozart. Both were popular and respected musicians in their time, and both remain among the best loved and most widely performed composers of our time. Haydn composed more than 100 symphonies and 68 string quartets, as well as sonatas, operas, masses, and other works. Although Mozart died just before he reached the age of 36, he composed more than 600 musical works, including over 40 symphonies and 20 concertos, which are considered among his greatest achievements.

A third major composer of the time, Ludwig van Beethoven, belongs both to the Classical period and to the next era, the Romantic period. Beethoven's compositions began in Classical style, but the texture, emotion, and new forms of his later music belong more to the Romantic period.

Check Your Understanding

Recall

1. To whom did artists of the Classical period look for standards and ideals?

2. What were the central attitudes of the Classical period?

3. What is chamber music?

4. For which instruments is a string quartet composed?

5. What is a symphony? Which four movements are usually included in a Classical symphony?

6. Who are the two major composers of the Classical period? What kinds of works did each compose?

Thinking It Through

1. Describe a Classical composition you have listened to. What characteristics mark the work as coming from the Classical period?

2. What do you think led Classical composers, other artists, and society in general to want less freedom and more structure?

Listening to . . .
Classical Music

CHORAL SELECTION

Mozart — *Don Giovanni*, Act I, "Là Ci Darem la Mano"

Born in Salzburg, Austria, Wolfgang Amadeus Mozart (1756–1791), whose full name is Johann Chrysostom Wolfgang Theophilus, began his musical career at an extremely early age. By the time he was four years old, Mozart had already mastered the keyboard and by age five had written his first musical piece. He became a master of the violin quickly thereafter. Mozart's father, Leopold Mozart, recognized Amadeus's talent and began a tour through Europe, exhibiting his son's extraordinary abilities. By age 16, Mozart had already written nearly 25 symphonies.

Don Giovanni is an opera in two acts. The characters are: Don Giovanni, a young nobleman; Leporello, his servant; the Commendatore Seville; Donna Anna, Seville's daughter; Don Ottavio, her fiancé; Donna Elvira, a lady of Burgos; Zerlina, a country girl; and Masetto, her fiancé.

In this aria, "Là Ci Darem la Mano," Don Giovanni sings to Zerlina, whom he meets at her engagement party. His flirtation is interrupted by the entrance of Donna Elvira, an old flame he had deserted. In the end of the opera, he receives just retribution for his actions when a supernatural fire destroys him and his palace.

INSTRUMENTAL SELECTION

Haydn — Symphony No. 94 in G major (*Surprise*)

Franz Joseph Haydn (1732–1809), a child prodigy and nine-year member of the Vienna Boys' Choir, spent most of his adult life working for Prince Esterhazy in Austria. While there, he wrote music for many occasions and experimented with music in new and different ways. He composed new forms and introduced touches of folk and gypsy music that he picked up from the country people. He was close friends with Mozart and was one of Beethoven's teachers. The *Surprise Symphony* was written for an evening concert after a dinner party. He put the loud (surprise) chord in to wake up the too-full, sleepy audience.

CLASSICAL CONNECTIONS

Introducing...

"Holy, Holy, Holy"

Wolfgang Amadeus Mozart

Setting the Stage

The most impressive feature of "Holy, Holy, Holy" is its overall clarity. You will see an uncluttered page, relatively simple rhythms, and a very chordal structure—all features of the Classical period. Also notice that the dynamic requirements are very precise and clearly defined between forte and piano, with no indications of crescendo or diminuendo. This is not to imply that there is not to be a musical "arch to the phrase" in the performance; it merely means that the style of the period does not include the highly emotional "rise-and-fall" that marks the music of the Romantic period.

Listen perceptively and you will hear all the elements coming together to create a clean, crisp style that is unmistakably Mozart!

Meeting the Composer
Wolfgang Amadeus Mozart

Mozart (1756–1791) is very familiar to all musicians for his many compositions in virtually every performance medium, from concerto to opera to symphony. He was a gifted child, and from the age of five he began to write music of such quality that it astounded the adults around him. As with many gifted individuals, he was misunderstood and did not receive the recognition he deserved while he was alive. His contributions to music history have now been duly noted and Mozart is ranked alongside Bach, Beethoven, and Brahms as one of the greatest composers to have ever lived.

CLASSICAL LESSON

Holy, Holy, Holy

COMPOSER: *Wolfgang Amadeus Mozart* (1756–1791)
ARRANGER: *Arthur Hardwicke*
ENGLISH TEXT: *Arthur Hardwicke*

CHORAL MUSIC TERMS
contrast
da capo
dynamics
fine
forte
homophony
marcato
piano
polyphony (imitation)
staccato

VOICING

SSA

PERFORMANCE STYLE

Adagio
Accompanied by piano or organ

FOCUS

- Identify and perform contrasting dynamics.
- Sing in three parts with homophonic and polyphonic (imitative) textures.
- Sing correct Latin pronunciation.

Warming Up

Vocal Warm-Up

Sing this warm-up using the text provided. Notice the stressed and marcato-staccato markings, and use your diaphragm to make this articulation happen. Keep your throat relaxed and jaw free at all times.

Neh- ah, neh- ah, neh- ah, neh- ah, neh- ah, neh- ah, neh- ah, neh- ah, neh.

Sight-Singing

Sight-sing this exercise using solfège and hand signs or numbers, with solid style and well-defined dynamics. How would you describe the movement of voice parts in relationship to one another? Is it consistent throughout the exercise? Notice the indication at the end to go back to the beginning (*da capo*) and sing to the double bar (*Fine*, meaning end).

Singing: "Holy, Holy, Holy"

Compare the sound of a basketball and a golf ball, both bounced with the same amount of energy on the same surface. Which sound would you call *forte*? Which would you call *piano*?

The amount of sound for piano and forte may differ, but the amount of breath support remains the same.

Now turn to the music for "Holy, Holy, Holy" on page 134.

HOW DID YOU DO?

?
•
?

With lots of support, you have learned this classical piece by Mozart. Think about your preparation and performance of "Holy, Holy, Holy."

1. Describe the dynamics in "Holy, Holy, Holy" and tell how they are or are not characteristic of Classical period style.

2. How is your Latin pronunciation? What is easy? What needs more work?

3. Describe the vocal textures included in "Holy, Holy, Holy," pointing them out in the notation. How are these related to the dynamics indicated for the piece?

Holy, Holy, Holy
(Sanctus)

Wolfgang Amadeus Mozart
Edited and arr. by Arthur Hardwicke
English text by A.H.

SSA with Piano or Organ Accompaniment

Ho - ly, Ho - ly,   Ho - ly
San - ctus, San - ctus,   Do - mi -

Ho - ly, Ho - ly,   Ho - ly Lord,   Ho - ly
San - ctus, San - ctus,   Do - mi - nus,   Do - mi -

Ho - ly, Ho - ly,   Ho - ly
San - ctus, San - ctus,   Do - mi -

Lord,   Ho - ly God of Sa - ba -
nus   De - us, De - us Sa - ba -

Lord,   Ho - ly God of Sa - ba -
nus   De - us, De - us Sa - ba -

Lord,   Ho - ly God of Sa - ba -
nus   De - us, De - us Sa - ba -

king-doms,   king-doms shall show forth Thy glo - ry.
ple - ni,   ple - ni sunt coe - li et ter - ra.

king-doms,   king-doms shall show forth Thy glo - ry.
ple - ni,   ple - ni sunt coe - li et ter - ra.

show forth Thy   glo - ry, shall show forth Thy glo - ry.
coe - li et   ter - ra, sunt coe - li et ter - ra.

Show _____ forth Thy glo - ry,
Glo - ri - a _ tu - a,

Show _____ forth Thy glo - ry,
Glo - ri - a tu - a,

Show _____ forth Thy glo - ry,
Glo - ri - a tu - a,

p

Ho - san - na   in
Ho - san - na   in

Ho - san - na   in
Ho - san - na   in

Ho - san - na   in
Ho - san - na   in

the   high - est,   Ho - san - na
ex - cel - sis,   Ho - san - na

the   high - est,   Ho - san - na
ex - cel - sis,   Ho - san - na

the   high - est,   Ho - san - na
ex - cel - sis,   Ho - san - na

in   the   high   -   est,   Ho - san - na
in   ex - cel   -   sis,   Ho - san - na

in   the   high   -   est,   Ho - san - na
in   ex - cel   -   sis,   Ho - san - na

in   the   high   -   est,   Ho - san - na
in   ex - cel   -   sis,   Ho - san - na

in   the   high   -   est.
in   ex - cel   -   sis.

in   the   high   -   est.
in   ex - cel   -   sis.

in   the   high   -   est.
in   ex - cel   -   sis.

An episode in the lives of the middle and lower classes of the nineteenth century is reflected in the realism of *Concert in the Tuileries* by Edouard Manet (1832–1883). The realistic treatment is also obvious in the dramatic subject matter that appeared in the operas of the Italian composers of the Romantic period, such as Rossini, Bellini, and Verdi.

1862. Edouard Manet. *Concert in the Tuileries.* (*Detail.*) Oil on canvas. 75 x 118 cm (30 x 46¹/₂"). National Gallery, London.

Romantic Period

After completing this lesson, you will be able to:

- Discuss the most important developments of the Romantic period.
- Identify the major musical forms of the Romantic period.
- Explain the importance of nationalism in Romantic music.
- Identify at least three major Romantic composers.

Emotion, imagination, and a concern for the individual returned to the arts with the Romantic period, which defined most of the nineteenth century, from about 1820 until around 1900. A new sense of political and artistic freedom emerged, as artists, including musicians, became impatient with established rules and tradition.

A Time of Freedom and Imagination

In many ways, the Romantic period was a reaction against the constraints of the Classical period. People became less interested in the balance and clarity of earlier times. Rather, their interests focused on adventure, a love of nature, and freedom of expression.

The Romantic period coincided with the Industrial Revolution, which created many new nonagricultural jobs and contributed to the growth of cities. The middle class grew in numbers, as well as in confidence and power. More and more people took an active part in their culture and their nation. A new sense of patriotism grew among citizens of individual European countries and of the United States.

Visual artists of the Romantic period reflected the era's attitudes with bolder, more colorful works. The enthusiasm for nature was reflected in the growing popularity of landscape paintings. The Romantic paintings of William Turner and John Constable express the movements and moods of nature. Later, Impressionist painters, including Edouard Manet, Claude Monet, and Pierre Auguste Renoir, developed new techniques to bring the sense and feeling of nature alive for the viewer.

Romantic Musical Developments

Romantic composers worked primarily with the same forms that had developed and become popular during the Classical period. However, Romantic composers treated these forms in ways that made new statements about music and about their own attitudes toward life. Romantic compositions, focused on both the heights and depths of human emotion, were characterized by complexity, exploration, and excitement. The interests of the period were expressed in larger, more complex vocal melodies and more colorful harmonies. In addition, instrumentation was expanded to enhance the overall possibilities of tone color in the music, and the rhythms became more free and more flexible.

COMPOSERS

Ludwig van Beethoven (1770–1827)
Franz Schubert (1797–1828)
Hector Berlioz (1803–1869)
Felix Mendelssohn (1809–1847)
Frédéric Chopin (1810–1849)
Robert Schumann (1810–1856)
Franz Liszt (1811–1886)
Richard Wagner (1813–1883)
Giuseppe Verdi (1813–1901)
Clara Schumann (1819–1896)
Johann Strauss (1825–1899)
Johannes Brahms (1833–1897)
Peter Ilyich Tschaikovsky (1840–1893)
Giacomo Puccini (1858–1924)

ARTISTS

Élisabeth Vigée-Lebrun (1755–1842)
Joseph Mallard William Turner (1775–1851)
John Constable (1776–1837)
Rosa Bonheur (1822–1899)
Edouard Manet (1832–1883)
James A. McNeill Whistler (1834–1903)
Edgar Degas (1834–1917)
Paul Cezanne (1839–1906)
Claude Monet (1840–1926)
Berthe Morisot (1841–1895)
Pierre Auguste Renoir (1841–1919)
Mary Cassatt (1845–1926)
Vincent van Gogh (1853–1890)
Georges Seurat (1859–1891)

AUTHORS

Noah Webster (1758–1843)
Sir Walter Scott (1771–1832)
Mary Wollstonecraft Shelley (1797–1851)
Ralph Waldo Emerson (1803–1882)

CHORAL MUSIC TERMS

art song
music critic
nationalism

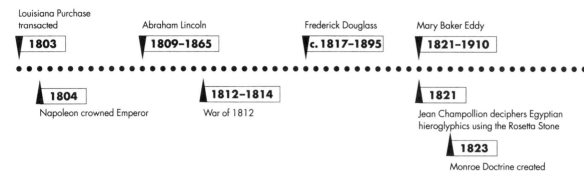

Louisiana Purchase
transacted
▼ 1803

Abraham Lincoln
▼ 1809–1865

Frederick Douglass
◄ c. 1817–1895

Mary Baker Eddy
▼ 1821–1910

▲ 1804
Napoleon crowned Emperor

▲ 1812–1814
War of 1812

▲ 1821
Jean Champollion deciphers Egyptian
hieroglyphics using the Rosetta Stone

▲ 1823
Monroe Doctrine created

Many Romantic compositions reflect the period's spirit of **nationalism**, *pride in a country's historical and legendary past*. Composers used traditional legends, as well as nationalistic dramas and novels, as the basis for both vocal and instrumental works.

Nationalism is seen perhaps most clearly in the operas of Richard Wagner and Giuseppe Verdi. Wagner's works, including the series of four operas known as *The Ring of the Nibelung*, are based on epic sagas and are intended to preserve German legends and folk music. Verdi, who has become the most popular of all opera composers, emphasized the importance of following Italian historical and cultural traditions.

Other musical forms of the Romantic period also reflect the era's nationalism. There was an increased interest in the traditional folk tunes and folk dances of specific nations or regions; these folk tunes were often used or imitated in serious compositions. German folk songs can be heard in Robert Schumann's piano pieces and symphonies, for example. In the United States, the songs composed by Stephen Foster express his understanding of and special pride in the southern United States.

As the Romantic period progressed, the most important vocal form became the **art song**, *an expressive song about life, love, and human relationships for solo voice and piano*. Art songs are known in German as *lieder*, and the most famous composers of these Romantic works were German-speakers. Austrian Franz Schubert composed more than 600 songs, as well as symphonies, string quartets, and other works, before his death at the age of 31. German composers Robert Schumann and Johannes Brahms are also known for their *lieder*.

Instrumental music became more elaborate and expressive during the Romantic period. Symphonies gained in popularity. Symphony orchestras increased in size, and percussion held a new place of importance. The most famous symphonies of the period—and perhaps of all time—are those composed by Ludwig van Beethoven. Some symphonies, including Beethoven's *Ninth Symphony*, added a chorus to the instrumental music.

Dance music also grew in importance during this time. Great social occasions became popular and required new dance compositions. The waltzes of Johann Strauss were played throughout Europe; new polonaises and other dance forms were also composed.

Modern Innovations of the Romantic Period

During the Romantic period, musicians and other artists received less support from wealthy or aristocratic patrons. As a result, composers began to think about "selling" their music to an audience. For several Romantic musicians, a colorful and controversial private life was part of "the package"; it sparked public interest in the composer and his works.

Another innovation of the period was the emergence of the **music critic**, *a writer who explains composers and their music to the public and who helps set standards in musical taste*. As music became more diverse and as increasing numbers of people listened to and appreciated new compositions, critics often sought to guide the direction new music might take.

Mary Mason Lyon founds Mt. Holyoke Female Seminary	American Civil War	Wireless telegraph developed by Guglielmo Marconi
1837	**1861–1865**	**1895**

1835–1910	**1844–1900**	**1889**	**1898**
Mark Twain	Friedrich Nietzsche	Jane Addams and Ellen Starr found Hull House	Motion picture camera patented by Thomas Edison; sound recording developed

▲ **John Nash (1752–1835) reaches for originality in his design of the Royal Pavilion in Brighton, England. The combination of Oriental onion domes and minarets with an interior in the Classical style is totally unique. Interest in the exotic was also a hallmark of Romantic composers who dealt with foreign lands as well as legends and mysticism in their works.**

1815–23. John Nash. Royal Pavilion, Brighton, England.

Check Your Understanding

Recall

1. In what ways was the Romantic period a reaction against the Classical period?

2. What is nationalism? How is it important in Romantic music?

3. What are art songs? Which Romantic composers are especially noted for this kind of composition?

4. How did symphonies change during the Romantic period?

5. Why did composers of the Romantic period have to start thinking about "selling" their music to an audience?

6. What is a music critic?

Thinking It Through

1. Review what you know about the musical ideals of the Renaissance period, the Baroque period, the Classical period, and the Romantic period. What cycle or trend can you identify? What implications do you think that cycle or trend might have?

2. What relationship do you think might exist between the decline of the patronage system and the emergence of the music critic?

Listening to...

Romantic Music

CHORAL SELECTION

Verdi — *Rigoletto,* Act III, Quartet

Rigoletto was first performed at Venice on March 11, 1851. It was based on Victor Hugo's *Le Roi s'amuse.* Giuseppe Verdi (1813–1901) chose librettos that show his deep sense of theater. For his texts, he usually chose plays with dramatic situations and forceful confrontations. Many of the librettos of the early opera use condensed, violent stories interspersed with bloody elements. *Rigoletto* is such an example.

INSTRUMENTAL SELECTION

Schumann — Romance in G Minor for Violin and Piano No. 2

Clara Schumann (1819–1896) is universally regarded as one of the most distinguished musicians of the nineteenth century. She was admired in Europe as an outstanding pianist, but never acknowledged in her lifetime as the outstanding composer that she was. Her main works are solo pieces, variations, chamber music (including the selection you will hear, a lied written in 1855–1856), cadenzas for Mozart and Beethoven piano concertos, and one piano concerto.

ROMANTIC CONNECTIONS

Introducing...

"Grüss"

Felix Mendelssohn

Setting the Stage

The soaring piano introduction you will hear in "Grüss" brings an audience to the entry of the singers with an anticipation of movement, of being lifted upward in the melody of the song. One is not disappointed; the voices quickly move to the highest pitch of the entire piece in only the third measure of the vocal lines! This is Romantic music at its best, bringing one to heights before experiencing depths. While the rhythmic content of the piece is not difficult, the calculation of the phrases presents a great challenge. The singer is asked to sing relatively long phrases that contain wide leaps and demanding dynamics.

Meeting the Composer
Felix Mendelssohn

Felix Mendelssohn-Bartholdy (1809–1847) was a Romantic composer who was highly influenced by Classical ideals. An accomplished pianist, he wrote music for piano requiring fluent technique, but in an elegant, sensitive style that was not as flamboyant as other composers of his time. His works closely follow the standard musical forms of the Classical period—for example, the sonata, the concerto, and the symphony—giving Romantic themes to these established vehicles of composition.

ROMANTIC LESSON

Grüss

COMPOSER: *Felix Mendelssohn (1809–1847)*
ENGLISH TEXT: *J. Von Eichendorff*
EDITED BY: *Robert Carl*

CHORAL MUSIC TERMS

melodic leaps

melodic repetition

melodic steps

sections

teneramente

voice parts

VOICING

SA

PERFORMANCE STYLE

Teneramente, non legato
(sustained, but not connected)
Accompanied by piano

FOCUS

- Identify and sing melodic steps and leaps.
- Identify melodic repetition between voice parts and sections of a piece.
- Sing using correct German pronunciation.

Warming Up

Vocal Warm-Up

Sing this warm-up using the text. Make sure to enunciate clearly throughout this exercise, using effective breath support. Tune the pitches carefully—especially on the big leaps.

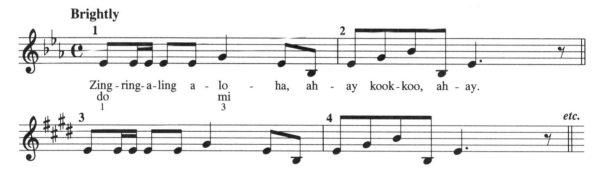

Sight-Singing

Sight-sing this exercise with a flowing style, using solfège and hand signs or numbers. How would you describe this melodic line? Do you find any repetition within this exercise?

Singing: "Grüss"

Echoes (or repetition) are a fundamental element of musical composition. Working with a partner, say a sentence and have your partner repeat it as soon as you finish. Take turns practicing this skill.

Next, repeat the same process, but sing the short phrases, with the other person repeating as soon as the pattern is finished. Switch roles.

Now turn to the music for "Grüss" on page 150.

HOW DID YOU DO?

? ?

Is your singing merely imitation, or did you make decisions about your performance based on analysis? Think about your preparation and performance of "Grüss."
1. The melody of "Grüss" has steps and leaps. Point out what these look like in your voice part. Which is easier for you to sing? Why?
2. Describe the two types of melodic repetition that occur in "Grüss." Did the repetition help you learn the piece? How?

3. Assess your ability to sing in German with correct pronunciation.
4. Describe the musical and text characteristics of "Grüss" that give clues to the period in which it was written. Are there any characteristics that you have seen or heard in music of previous periods?

Grüss

(Greeting)

Felix Mendelssohn
(Op. 63, No. 3)
English Text by J. Von Eichendorff
Edited by Robert Carl

SA and Piano

Individuals in contemporary society are increasingly interested in expressing their ethnic backgrounds. Palmer Hayden (1890–1973) shows this interest by juxtaposing the comedy, tragedy, and pleasures of the African-American painter who works during the day as a janitor, yet aspires to be a great artist. Music of the twentieth century is influenced by many different cultures as well as by technology and experimentation.

1937. Palmer Hayden. *The Janitor Who Paints*. Oil on canvas. 99.4 x 83.5 cm (39 ¹/₈ x 32 ⁷/₈"). National Museum of American Art, Washington, D.C.

Contemporary Period

After completing this lesson, you will be able to:

- Identify technological advancements that have affected the involvement of the general public in the music of the Contemporary period.
- Discuss at least five musical developments of the Contemporary period.
- Identify at least four Contemporary composers.
- Explain the importance of fusion in Contemporary music.

The twentieth century has been a period of rapid change. The developments in transportation may typify the rate at which change has taken place in all aspects of modern life. In 1900, the first automobiles were coming into use, and the first successful airplane was yet to be built. Today, highways are jammed with automobiles, commercial flights take off regularly from large and small airports, and unmanned spaceflights explore the farthest reaches of the solar system.

Political events have brought repeated and often radical changes in the lives and ideas of people around the world. Among the major political events of the twentieth century have been two world wars, many localized wars, revolutions in Russia and China, the Great Depression, the Cold War, and the rise and fall of communism in many countries. All these changes and more have been part of the Contemporary period, the time from 1900 to right now.

Technology and Contemporary Music

Technological advancements have affected many aspects of twentieth-century life, including the musical interests and involvement of the general public. First, phonographs and records made music readily available to everyone who wanted to hear it. Then, radio brought live musical performances and a wide variety of musical recordings into people's homes. By now, television has replaced radio as a source of news and entertainment—including news about music and musical entertainment—in most homes. Audiotapes, CDs, and computers with interactive software have also become popular, bringing higher quality sounds and images to the public. In addition, synthesizers now make it easier and less expensive for everyone to become involved in making and listening to music.

During the Contemporary period, music and musicians have had to rely much more on the general public for support than during any past time. Composers or musicians may still be employed by religious

COMPOSERS

Richard Strauss (1864–1949)
Ralph Vaughan Williams (1872–1958)
Arnold Schoenberg (1874–1951)
Charles Ives (1874–1954)
Pablo Casals (1876–1973)
Béla Bartók (1881–1945)
Igor Stravinsky (1882–1971)
Sergei Prokofiev (1891–1953)
Bessie Smith (1894–1937)
Paul Hindemith (1895–1963)
George Gershwin (1898–1937)
Aaron Copland (1900–1990)
Samuel Barber (1910–1981)
Gian Carlo Menotti (1911–)
Benjamin Britten (1913–1976)
Leonard Bernstein (1918–1990)
Philip Glass (1937–)

ARTISTS

Henri Rousseau (1844–1910)
Edvard Munch (1863–1944)
Wassily Kandinsky (1866–1944)
Henri Matisse (1869–1954)
Pablo Picasso (1881–1973)
Georgia O'Keeffe (1887–1986)
Palmer Hayden (1890–1973)
Jackson Pollock (1912–1956)
Andrew Wyeth (1917–)
Andy Warhol (1930–1987)

AUTHORS

George Bernard Shaw (1856–1950)
Sir Arthur Conan Doyle (1859–1930)
Edith Wharton (1862–1937)

CHORAL MUSIC TERMS

abstract
aleatoric music
dissonance
Expressionism
fusion
Impressionism
twelve-tone music

Wright Brothers' flight

1903

Model T Ford introduced

1908

Leopold Stokowski named conductor of
the Philadelphia Symphony Orchestra

1912

1905

First motion picture
theater opens

1909

Sergei Diaghilev presents
"Ballet Russe" for the first
time in Paris

1914–1918

World War I

1919

Observations of the total eclipse
of the sun confirm Albert Einstein's
theory of relativity

organizations, city orchestras, or schools, but most support themselves through the sale of concert tickets, published music, and professional recordings. Music also receives some support from nonprofit organizations, but the era of the patronage system is clearly over.

Musical Developments of the Contemporary Period

The twentieth century has been a time of musical changes. Many composers have continued to use forms from the Romantic period, such as the opera, symphony, and art song, but they have adapted these forms to express new musical ideas. Many compositions from the early part of the century are considered **Impressionism**, *works that create a musical picture with a dreamy quality through chromaticism.* Many later works are considered examples of **Expressionism**, *bold and dynamic musical expression of mood with great dissonance.*

Composers of the Contemporary period have experimented with many different approaches to music. Some have worked in an objective style, creating works that stress music for its own sake. Their compositions are **abstract**, *focusing on lines, rows, angles, clusters, textures, and form.*

Many composers have also experimented with music that lacks a tonal center and a scale-oriented organization of pitch. Rather than using traditional chords built on intervals of a third, these modern compositions feature **dissonance**, *chords using seconds, fourths, fifths, and sevenths.*

Another new development is **twelve-tone music**. In this organization, *the twelve tones of the chromatic scale are arranged in a tone row, then the piece is composed by arranging and rearranging the "row" in different ways—backward, forward, in clusters of three or four pitches, and so on.* Twelve-tone compositions can be approached mathematically, and the possible combinations are nearly limitless, especially when arrangements are layered, instrument over instrument. Although this approach to composition fascinates some composers, not all listeners find the resulting works satisfying.

Some Contemporary composers have also created **aleatoric**—or chance—**music**, *works that have only a beginning and an end, with the rest left to chance.* An aleatoric work usually does have a score, but each performer is given the freedom to make many choices, including which pitch to begin on, how long to hold each pitch, how fast to play, and when to stop playing.

Other compositional elements of the Contemporary period include more angular contour of the melody, different concepts of harmony, which may emphasize dissonance, complex rhythms, and specific performance markings. These musical innovations are most evident in the secular music of the twentieth century, but they can be seen in many sacred works as well. The number of sacred compositions has decreased

First complete talking film	Television begins under commercial license	First atomic bomb exploded
1928	**1939**	**1945**

1927	**1929**	**1939–1945**	**1950–1953**
Lindbergh's solo flight across the Atlantic	New York stock market collapses; Great Depression begins	World War II	Korean War

▲ **Just as new compositional techniques in various formats are prevalent in Contemporary music, the architecture in the Opera House in Sydney, Australia, incorporated new materials and construction techniques. Award-winning Danish architect Jørn Utzon (1918–) called for segmented, precast concrete in the construction of the white tiled shells that form the roof of this imaginative and poetic building.**

1959–72. Jørn Utzon. Opera House, Sydney, Australia.

during this century. However, important Contemporary musicians, including Leonard Bernstein, Paul Hindemith, Benjamin Britten, Charles Ives, and Gian Carlo Menotti, have composed masses, sacred cantatas, chorales, and othe religious works.

A New Mix

Rapid improvements in communication and transportation have brought people from all parts of the world into closer touch with one another. Individuals and groups have shared many aspects of their cultures, including traditional musical techniques and new musical developments. One of the results of this sharing is **fusion**, *a blending*

Contemporary Period **159**

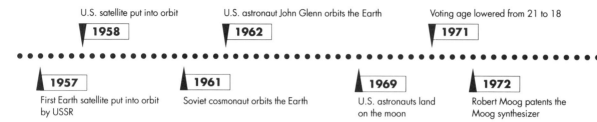

U.S. satellite put into orbit
1958

U.S. astronaut John Glenn orbits the Earth
1962

Voting age lowered from 21 to 18
1971

1957
First Earth satellite put into orbit
by USSR

1961
Soviet cosmonaut orbits the Earth

1969
U.S. astronauts land
on the moon

1972
Robert Moog patents the
Moog synthesizer

of musical styles. Tejano music, for example, is a blending of Mexican and Country styles; zydeco is a blending of African-American, Cajun, and French Canadian styles.

The Contemporary period has also been a time of fusion between popular music styles and art music. Pop singers occasionally perform with professional orchestras and choirs, and opera singers record popular songs and traditional folk music.

Many new kinds of popular music have emerged during the Contemporary period. Some, including blues, jazz, country, rock, and reggae, continue to thrive and to blend with other kinds of popular music. Other styles, such as ragtime, seem to have become part of history rather than popular culture. Popular music styles are part of the change characteristic of the period, and new styles will continue to develop.

The Future of Music

The changes of the Contemporary period are ongoing, and the music of the period continues to evolve. Which trends will prove most significant? When will a new direction emerge that will mark the end of this period? What name will future historians give to the time we call Contemporary? As a consumer of music—and perhaps even as a music maker—you may help determine the answers to these questions.

Check Your Understanding

Recall

1. What is Impressionism?

2. What is abstract music?

3. What is dissonance?

4. List at least three choices that are left up to performers of aleatoric music.

5. What is the status of sacred music in the Contemporary period?

6. What is fusion? Give at least two examples of fusion.

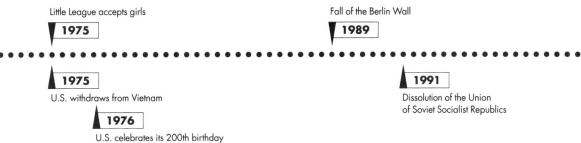

Little League accepts girls

1975

U.S. withdraws from Vietnam

1975

U.S. celebrates its 200th birthday

1976

Fall of the Berlin Wall

1989

Dissolution of the Union
of Soviet Socialist Republics

1991

Thinking It Through

1. How do you think the change from a patronage system to a reliance on public support has affected the development of music? Explain your ideas.

2. What forms of Contemporary music do you like best? Why? Be specific.

3. Which previous period—Renaissance, Baroque, Classical, or Romantic—do you consider most like the Contemporary period? What similarities can you identify? What do you consider the most important differences?

Listening to...
Contemporary Music

CHORAL SELECTION

Smith—"Lost Your Head Blues"

Bessie Smith (1894–1937) was known as the "Empress of the Blues." Raised in an impoverished background, she became famous for singing of hopelessness and despair. Tragically, she died of complications from an auto accident after being turned away from a white hospital in this period of rigid segregation. She died en route to a black hospital in Mississippi.

INSTRUMENTAL SELECTION

Stravinsky—*Firebird* Suite, Scene 2

Igor Stravinsky (1882–1971) is considered one of the most influential composers of the 1900s. His most famous works include *The Firebird*, *Petrouchka*, and *The Rite of Spring*. Since *The Firebird* is a ballet based on a Russian legend, many versions of the story can be found. The basic fairy tale begins with Prince Ivan, the Czar's son, hunting in a forest. He captures a magical golden bird with wings of fire. The firebird gives Ivan a feather in return for its freedom. Ivan continues his walk through the woods when suddenly he sees King Katschei's castle. The evil King has turned many prisoners into stone and is holding princesses as captives. Ivan enters the sinister castle. With the help of the magic feather, he conquers King Katschei, the castle sinks into the ground, and the 13 princesses and prisoners are freed. Prince Ivan falls in love with one of the princesses and, as in most fairy tales, they live happily ever after.

CONTEMPORARY CONNECTIONS

Introducing...

"Nigra Sum"

Pablo Casals

Setting the Stage

Though composers of the twentieth century are constantly seeking new ways to present musical composition, there are also the traditionalists. These composers are recognized for their creativity based on traditional harmonies: harmonies with some twentieth-century dissonance, but not a far stretch from the harmonies enjoyed by the composers of the Romantic period. Casals demonstrates such traditionalism in this work; Neo-Romantic is its basic style. However, the Neo-Romantic composers used percussion more predominately. This work of Casals, "Nigra Sum," is written for piano and choir, and the choir has all the rich quality of the cello, cast in lyricism rather than percussive verticalism.

Meeting the Composer
Pablo Casals

Pablo Casals is known as one of the great Spanish cellists. He was born in Vendrell, Catalonia, on December 29, 1876. He died in San Juan, Puerto Rico, on October 22, 1973. His father, the parish organist and choirmaster in Vendrell, gave Casals instruction in piano, violin, and organ. When Casals was eleven, he first heard the cello performed by a group of traveling musicians and decided to study the instrument. In 1888, his mother took him to Barcelona, where he enrolled in Escuela Municipal de Música. There, his progress as a cellist was nothing short of prodigious and he gave a solo recital in Barcelona at the age of fourteen. By 1956, he had moved to San Juan, Puerto Rico, which became his permanent home.

Winner of the United Nations Peace Prize, Casals played at the General Assembly Hall in 1958 to celebrate the United Nations' thirteenth anniversary. In 1961, he performed for President Kennedy at the White House. Many significant twentieth-century works have been dedicated to him, and the Monks of Montserrat perform his sacred works extensively, valuing their simplicity, conviction, and traditional style.

Nigra Sum

COMPOSER: *Pablo Casals* (1876–1973)
ENGLISH TEXT: *Kenneth Sterne*

CHORAL MUSIC TERMS
breathing
pitch
posture
rhythm

VOICING
Three-part chorus

PERFORMANCE STYLE
Moderato
Accompanied by piano or organ

FOCUS
- Read and sing familiar rhythms and pitches using a rich tone quality.
- Use correct posture and breathing.
- Sing using correct Latin pronunciation.

Warming Up

Vocal Warm-Up
Using rich vocal tones, sing this warm-up on *yah-oh-e-ah*. Take a deep breath and concentrate on singing tall vowels, providing a lot of room toward the back of the mouth. Hold your index finger about an inch from your lips and feel the warm air the tone is using. If the air is cool, the breath was shallow. If the air is warm the breath was deep. Move up or down by half steps on the repeat.

Sight-Singing

Sight-sing this exercise using solfège and hand signs or numbers. Sing the pitches richly. The melody is easy so you are free to concentrate on the tone you are producing. Make your voice sound like a cello.

Singing: "Nigra Sum"

Can you tell, just by looking, if an athlete is good? What clues might you look for? Can you tell, just by looking, if a singer is good? What clues might you look for?

Now turn to the music for "Nigra Sum" on page 166.

Now turn to the music for "Nigra Sum" on page 166.

HOW DID YOU DO?

?

If someone were watching you sing, would that person know if you are a good singer? Think about your preparation and performance of "Nigra Sum."

1. Did you use correct posture and breathing? How would the observer know? What would they see? What do you feel?

2. Could you read the rhythms and pitches of the piece? What was easy? What needed practice?

3. Was your Latin pronunciation correct? What was good? What could be better?

4. Could you make your voice sound rich like a cello? How did you do it?

Nigra Sum

I am Black

(Decepta ex Canticis)

Pablo Casals
English version by Kenneth Sterne

Three-part Chorus of Treble Voices
with Piano or Organ Accompaniment

A. B. 120

A.B. 120

A.B. 120

Nigra Sum **171**

A.B. 120

Additional Performance Selections

VOICING

Two-part chorus

PERFORMANCE STYLE

Vivace
Accompanied by piano or organ

Gloria

Warming Up

Vocal Warm-Up

Sing this exercise using solfège and hand signs or numbers. Then sing it using the text provided. Sing it with a good bounce on the breath. There's plenty of action for both consonants and vowels. Move up by half steps as you repeat. Notice that this is the main theme of "Gloria."

Zing-ring-a-ling, a-lo-ha, eh - ah.

Now turn to page **180**.

VOICING

Three-part treble voices

PERFORMANCE STYLE

Andante
Accompanied by harp or piano

I Wonder As I Wander

Warming Up

Vocal Warm-Up

Sing this exercise using solfège and hand signs or numbers, then on *loo*. Move up by half steps on each repeat. This will give you a feel for the tonality and meter of "I Wonder As I Wander."

Slowly

Loo

Now turn to page **187**.

VOICING

SSAA

PERFORMANCE STYLE

With feeling
Accompanied by flute

Native American Spring Songs

Warming Up

Vocal Warm-Up

Sing this exercise tuning the parallel thirds carefully. Sing one vowel sound for each note, keeping each vowel completely focused throughout the exercise. Use a deep breath to expand your waistline, which you can feel by putting your hands on your sides, turned toward your stomach.

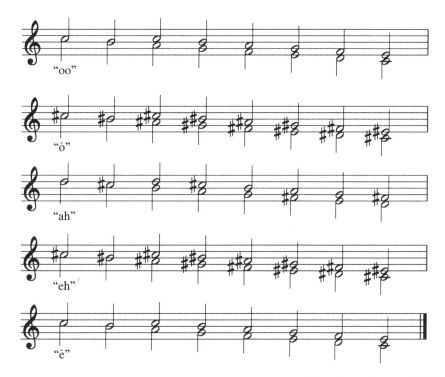

Now turn to page **196.**

VOICING
Unison or two-part choir

PERFORMANCE STYLE
With sparkle
Accompanied by keyboard

Festival Alleluia

Warming Up

Vocal Warm-Up
Sing this exercise using solfège and hand signs or numbers, swaying to the two beats felt in each measure. Notice the 6/8 meter. Move up by half steps on each repeat.

do re mi
1 2 3

Now turn to page **201.**

VOICING
SSA

PERFORMANCE STYLE
Excitedly
A cappella

Wisdom and Understanding

Warming Up

Vocal Warm-Up
Sing this exercise using each vowel (a, e, i, o, u) for the whole exercise, then use the next vowel, moving up or down a half step. First get the pitches tuned in each chord. Then work on choral blend by singing uniform vowels. Keep each vowel focused through the lower, middle, and upper range.

1. Ah
2. Eh
3. ee
4. ō
5. o͞o

Now turn to page **207.**

VOICING

SSA

PERFORMANCE STYLE

Sprightly
Accompanied by piano

Beautiful Yet Truthful

Warming Up

Vocal Warm-Up

Sing this exercise using solfège and hand signs or numbers. Move up or down by half steps. Sing it faster and faster, but articulate the syllables with the utmost precision. Find this pattern in "Beautiful Yet Truthful." Is it exactly the same?

Now turn to page **214.**

Gloria

From the Heiligmesse (1796)

Joseph Haydn (1732–1809)
Edited by Bennett Williams

Two-part Chorus (SA or TB) Piano or Organ

Glo-ri-a in ex-cel-sis De - o,
Glory to God in heav - en, glo - ry!

Glo-ri-a in ex-cel-sis,
Glo-ry to God in heav - en,

Glo-ri-a in ex-cel-sis De - o,
Glory to God in heav - en, glo - ry!

Glo-ri-a in ex-cel-sis,
Glo-ry to God in heav - en,

I Wonder As I Wander

Appalachian Carol
Arranged and adapted by Richard Osborne

Three-part Treble Voices with Harp

come for to die for poor orn - 'ry peo - ple like you and like

come for to die for poor orn - 'ry peo - ple like you and like

come for to die for poor orn - 'ry peo - ple like you and like

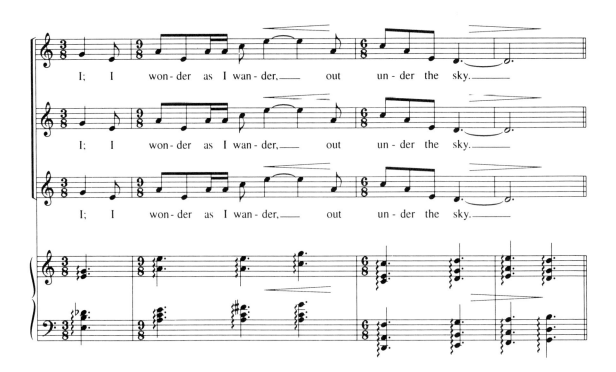

I; I won-der as I wan-der,___ out un-der the sky.___

I; I won-der as I wan-der,___ out un-der the sky.___

I; I won-der as I wan-der,___ out un-der the sky.___

high from God's heav - en a star's light did fall, The

high from God's heav - en a star's light did fall, The

high from God's heav - en a star's light did fall, The

prom - ise of a - ges_____ it then did re - call._____

prom - ise of a - ges_____ it then did re - call._____

prom - ise of a - ges_____ it then did re - call._____

star in the sky or a bird on the wing, Or

star in the sky or a bird on the wing, Or

loo   Or

all of God's an - gels in heav'n for to sing. He

all of God's an - gels in heav'n for to sing. He

all of God's an - gels in heav'n for to sing. He

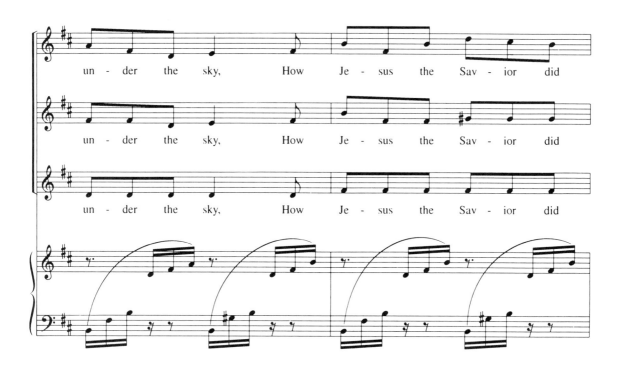

un - der the sky, How Je - sus the Sav - ior did

un - der the sky, How Je - sus the Sav - ior did

un - der the sky, How Je - sus the Sav - ior did

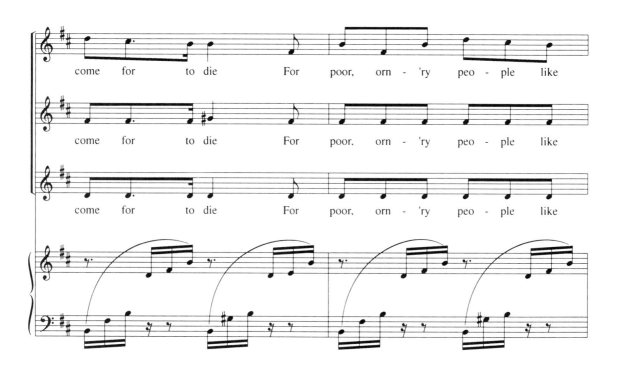

come for to die For poor, orn - 'ry peo - ple like

come for to die For poor, orn - 'ry peo - ple like

come for to die For poor, orn - 'ry peo - ple like

you and like I; I won-der as I wan-der,——— out

you and like I; I won-der as I wan-der,——— out

you and like I; I won-der as I wan-der,——— out

Rallentando

un - der the sky. loo————

un - der the sky. loo————

un - der the sky. loo————

Rallentando

Native American Spring Songs
1. As My Eyes Search

Chippewa
By Nancy Grundahl

2. All Winter Long

By Nancy Grundahl

Where did we run, run_____ be - yond gate and guardsman?

Where did we run,_____ run_____ be - yond gate and guardsman?

Guess if you can,_____ we ran_____ to the sun,____

Guess if you can,_____ we ran_____ to the sun,____

the dance_____ of the sun._____

the dance_____ of the sun._____

accel.

For the Greater Detroit Chapter Choristers Guild

Festival Alleluía

Allen Pote

Unison or Two-part Choir with Keyboard

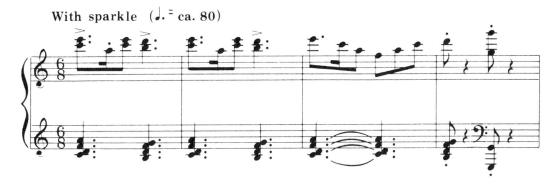

With sparkle (♩. = ca. 80)

mf

Sing ____ un - to God ____ all the heav-ens and earth, ____

____ Al - le - lu - ia, clap your hands, *(clap, clap)* re - joice and

sing a joy - ful song. Sing it loud - ly,

sing it mer - ri - ly, _____ sing it soft - ly,

sing with a beau - ti - ful mel - o - dy.

Sing ___ un - to God ___ all the heav-ens and earth, ___ Al-le-lu - ia,

cel - e-brate, *(snap, snap)* and with a cheer - ful voice sing

al - le - lu - ia, sing it from your heart.

Make your life a song to God.

with articulation

Lis-ten to the rhy-thm, to the rhy-thm of cre-a-tion,

listen to the beat of life.___ Wake up to the won-der of a world in cel-e-bra-tion,

wake up to a world of light,___ and sing, chil-dren, sing al-le-lu-ia,___

praise to the Lord a-bove. Sing, chil-dren, sing al-le-lu-ia,___ God___ is love.

Wisdom and Understanding

Kent A. Newbury
Job 28: 20–21, 23–28 (RSV)

SSA Chorus A cappella

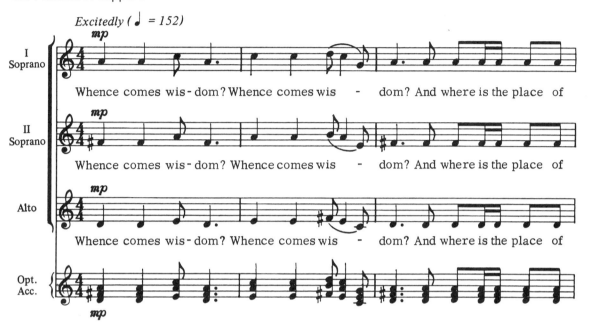

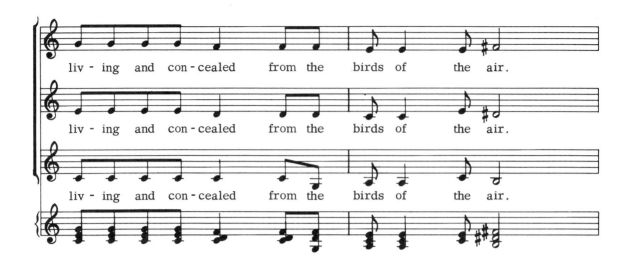

living and con-cealed from the birds of the air.

living and con-cealed from the birds of the air.

living and con-cealed from the birds of the air.

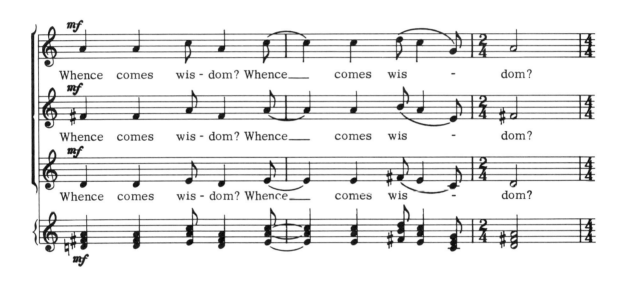

Whence comes wis-dom? Whence___ comes wis - dom?

Whence comes wis-dom? Whence___ comes wis - dom?

Whence comes wis-dom? Whence___ comes wis - dom?

God un-der-stands the way to it, And He knows___ its

God un-der-stands the way to it, And He knows___ its

God un-der-stands the way to it, And He knows___ its

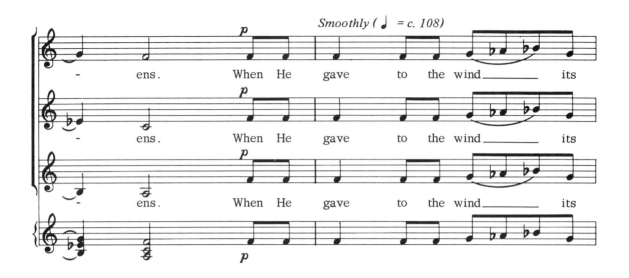

-ens. When He gave to the wind _____ its

-ens. When He gave to the wind _____ its

-ens. When He gave to the wind _____ its

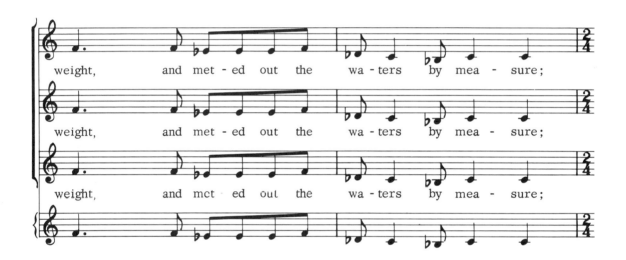

weight, and met - ed out the wa - ters by mea - sure;

weight, and met - ed out the wa - ters by mea - sure;

weight, and met - ed out the wa - ters by mea - sure;

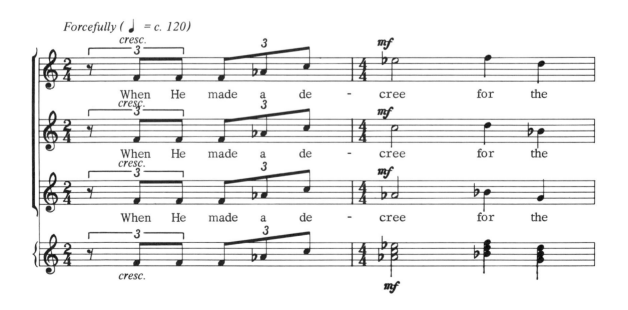

When He made a de - cree for the

When He made a de - cree for the

When He made a de - cree for the

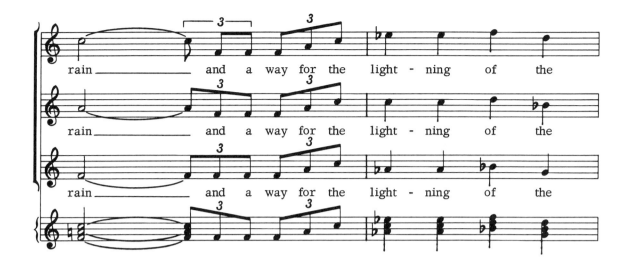

rain _____ and a way for the light - ning of the

rain _____ and a way for the light - ning of the

rain _____ and a way for the light - ning of the

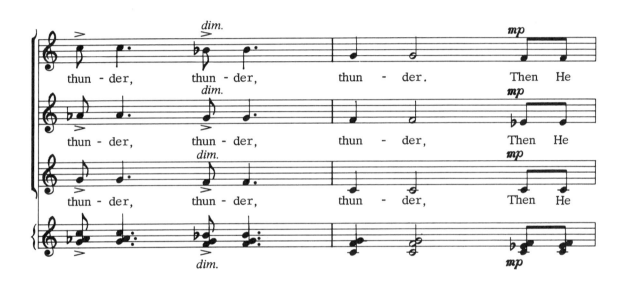

thun - der, thun - der, thun - der. Then He

thun - der, thun - der, thun - der, Then He

thun - der, thun - der, thun - der, Then He

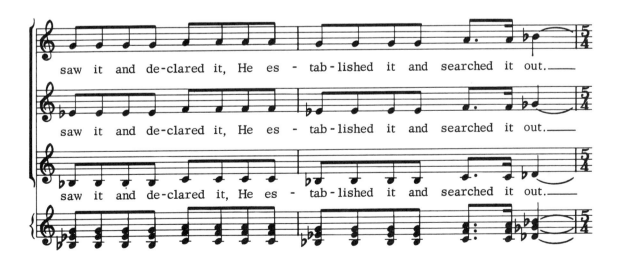

saw it and de-clared it, He es - tab - lished it and searched it out. ___

saw it and de-clared it, He es - tab - lished it and searched it out. ___

saw it and de-clared it, He es - tab - lished it and searched it out. ___

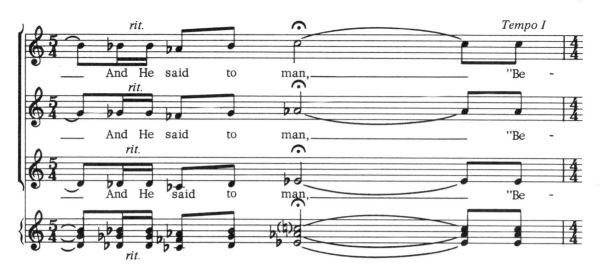

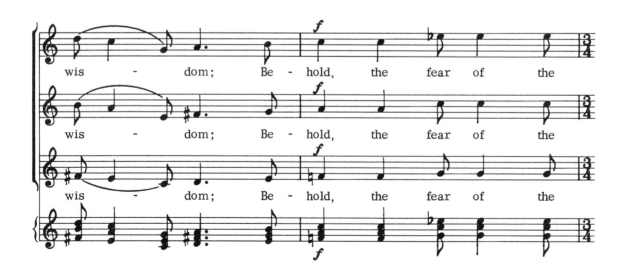

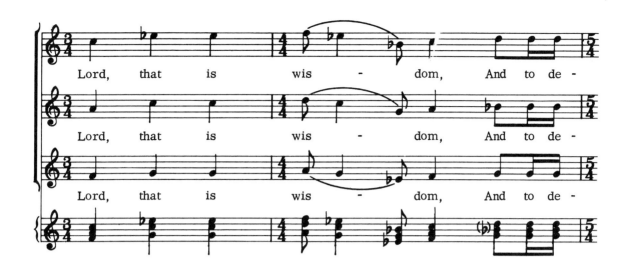

Lord, that is wis - dom, And to de-

part from e - vil is un - der - stand - ing, un - der - stand - ing,

Wis - dom and un - der - stand - ing." That is wis - dom.

Beautiful Yet Truthful

A Folksong Elaboration*
By Lloyd Pfautsch

Three-part Chorus of Female Voices
with Piano Accompaniment

* From *American Ballads and Folksongs* by John Lomax, used by permission

rar - in', tear - in' beau - ti-ful? I ain't got no peace of mind,

Ev'-ry-bod-y is so aw-ful-ly kind. Out-side of my door they

stand, stand, Wait-in' for my heart and hand. Out-side of my door they

stand, stand, Wait-in' for my heart and hand.——— Al-most ev'-ry

rar-in', tear-in', brain-y! Ain't it fierce to be so brain-y, brain-y,

rar-in', tear-in', brain-y! Ain't it fierce to be so brain-y, brain-y,

Ain't it fierce to be so brain-y! I ain't got no

Ain't it fierce to be so brain-y! I ain't got no

peace of mind, The teach-ers are so aw-ful-ly kind, Our-

peace of mind, The teach-ers are so aw-ful-ly kind, Out-

Ain't it fierce___

Ain't it fierce___

Ain't it fierce___

Slower ♩ = 60
mp

(for rebearsal only)

___ to be so truth - ful, truth - ful?

___ to be so truth - ful, truth - ful?

___ to be so — truth - ful, truth - ful?

Ain't it fierce to be so truth - - - ful?

Ain't it fierce to be so truth - ful?

Ain't it fierce to be so truth - ful!

Ev'-ry-one says my hon-es-ty — Is on - ly matched by my

Ev'-ry-one says my hon-es-ty Is on - ly matched by my

Ev'-ry-one says my hon-es-ty Is on - ly matched by my

mo - des - ty. Oh, ain't it fierce to be so truth-ful, truth-ful?

mo - des - ty. Oh, ain't it fierce to be so truth-ful, truth-ful?

mo - des - ty. Oh, ain't it fierce to be so truth ful, truth-ful?

Ain't it fierce to be so truth - ful? Ain't it fierce to be so

Ain't it fierce to be so truth - ful? Ain't it fierce to be so

Ain't it fierce to be so truth - ful? Ain't it fierce to be so

truth-ful, truth-ful? Ain't it fierce___ to be beau-ti-ful,

truth-ful, truth-ful? Ain't it fierce___ to be beau-ti-ful,

truth-ful, truth-ful? Ain't it fierce___ to be beau-ti-ful,

brain-y yet truth - - - ful?

brain-y yet truth - - ful?

brain-y yet truth - - ful?

Bloomington, Illinois
March 12, 1955

Glossary

Choral Music Terms

A

a cappella (ah-kah-PEH-lah) [It.] Unaccompanied vocal music.

accelerando (*accel.*) (ah-chel-leh-RAHN-doh) [It.] Gradually increasing the tempo.

accent Indicates the note is to be sung with extra force or stress. (>)

accidentals Signs used to indicate the raising or lowering of a pitch. A sharp (♯) alters a pitch by raising it one-half step; a flat (♭) alters a pitch by lowering it one-half step; a natural (♮) cancels a sharp or a flat.

accompaniment Musical material that supports another; for example, a piano or orchestra accompanying a choir or soloist.

adagio (ah-DAH-jee-oh) [It.] Slow tempo, but not as slow as largo.

ad libitum (ad. lib.) [Lt.] An indication that the performer may vary the tempo, add or delete a vocal or instrumental part. Synonymous with a *piacere*.

al fine (ahl FEE-neh) [It.] To the end.

alla breve Indicates cut time; duple meter in which there are two beats per measure, the half note getting one beat. (¢)

allargando (*allarg.*) (ahl-ahr-GAHN-doh) [It.] To broaden, become slower.

aleatoric or chance music Music in which chance is deliberately used as a compositional component.

allegro (ah-LEH-groh) [It.] Brisk tempo; faster than moderato, slower than *vivace*.

allegro assai (ah-LEH-groh ah-SAH-ee) [It.] Very fast; in seventeenth-century music, the term can also mean "sufficiently fast."

altered pitch A note that does not belong to the scale of the work being performed.

alto The lower female voice; sometimes called contralto or mezzo-soprano.

anacrusis (a-nuh-KROO-suhs) [Gk.] *See* upbeat.

andante (ahn-DAHN-teh) [It.] Moderately slow; a walking tempo.

andante con moto (ahn-DAHN-teh kohn MOH-toh) [It.] A slightly faster tempo, "with motion."

animato Quick, lively; "animated."

anthem A choral composition in English using a sacred text. *See also* motet.

antiphonal Music performed by alternating ensembles, positioned in opposing locations, as in choirs or brass; first brought to prominence by Giovanni Gabrielli at St. Mark's Cathedral, Venice, in the Baroque period.

appassionato (uh-pah-shun-NAHT-oh) [It.] With deep feeling, passionately.

appoggiatura (uh-pah-zhuh-TOOR-uh) [It.] A nonharmonic tone, usually a half or whole step above the harmonic tone, performed on the beat, resolving downward to the harmonic tone.

aria (AHR-ee-uh) [It.] A song for a solo singer and orchestra, usually in an opera, oratorio, or cantata.

arpeggio (ahr-PEH-jee-oh) [It.] A chord in which the pitches are sounded successively, usually from lowest to highest; in broken style.

art song Expressive songs about life, love, and human relationships for solo voice and piano.

articulation Clarity in performance of notes and diction.

a tempo (ah TEM-poh) [It.] Return to the established tempo after a change.

atonality Music not organized around a key center.

augmentation A technique used in composition by which the melody line is repeated in doubled note values; opposite of *diminution*.

augmented The term indicating that a major or perfect interval has been enlarged by one-half step; as in C-F♯ (augmented fourth) or C-G♯ (augmented fifth).

B

balance and symmetry Even and equal.

baritone The male voice between tenor and bass.

bar line (measure bar) A vertical line drawn through the staff to show the end of a measure. Double bar lines show the end of a section or a piece of music.

Baroque period (buh-ROHK) [Fr.] Historic period between c. 1600 and c. 1750 that reflected highly embellished styles in art, architecture, fashion, manners, and music. The period of elaboration.

bass The lowest male voice, below tenor and baritone.

bass clef Symbol at the beginning of the staff for lower voices and instruments, or the piano left hand; usually referring to pitches lower than middle C. The two dots lie on either side of the fourth-line F, thus the term, F clef. 𝄢

beat A steady pulse.

bel canto   (bell KAHN-toh) [It.] Italian vocal technique of the eighteenth century with emphasis on beauty of sound and brilliance of performance.

binary form   Defines a form having two sections (A and B), each of which may be repeated.

bitonality   The designation of music written in two different keys at the same time.

breath mark   A mark placed within a phrase or melody showing where the singer or musician should breathe. (⸴)

C

cadence   Punctuation or termination of a musical phrase; a breathing break.

caesura   (si-ZHUR-uh) [Lt.] A break or pause between two musical phrases. (//)

call and response   A song style that follows a simple question-and-answer pattern in which a soloist leads and a group responds.

calypso style   Folk-style music from the Caribbean Islands with bright, syncopated rhythm.

cambiata   The young male voice that is still developing.

canon   A compositional form in which the subject is begun in one group and then is continually and exactly repeated by other groups. Unlike the round, the canon closes with all voices ending together on a common chord.

cantata   (kan-TAH-tuh) [It.] A collection of vocal compositions with instrumental accompaniment consisting of several movements based on related secular or sacred text segments.

cantabile   In a lyrical, singing style.

cantor   A solo singer in the Jewish and Roman Catholic traditions who leads the congregation in worship by introducing responses and other musical portions of the services.

cantus firmus   (KAHN-tuhs FUHR-muhs) [Lt.] A previously-composed melody which is used as a basis for a new composition.

chance music   See aleatoric music.

chantey   (SHAN-tee) [Fr.] A song sung by sailors in rhythm with their work.

chant, plainsong   Music from the liturgy of the early church, characterized by free rhythms, monophonic texture, and sung *a cappella*.

chorale   (kuh-RAL) [Gr.] Congregational song or hymn of the German Protestant (Evangelical) Church.

chord   Three or more pitches sounded simultaneously.

chord, block   Three or more pitches sounded simultaneously.

chord, broken   Three or more pitches sounded in succession; *see also* arpeggio.

chromatic   (kroh-MAT-ik) [Gr.] Moving up or down by half steps. Also the name of a scale composed entirely of half steps.

Classical period   The period in Western history beginning around 1750 and lasting until around 1820 that reflected a time when society began looking to the ancient Greeks and Romans for examples of order and ways of looking at life.

clef   The symbol at the beginning of the staff that identifies a set of pitches; *see also* bass clef and treble clef.

coda   Ending section; a concluding portion of a composition. (⊕)

common time   Another name for 4/4 meter; *see also* cut time. (**c**)

composer   The creator of musical works.

compound meter   Meter whose beat can be subdivided into threes and/or sixes.

con   (kohn) [It.] With.

con brio   (kohn BREE-oh) [It.] With spirit; vigorously.

concerto   Composition for solo instrument and an orchestra, usually with three movements.

con moto   (kohn MOH-toh) [It.] With motion.

consonance   A musical interval or chord that sounds pleasing; opposite of dissonance.

Contemporary period   The time from 1900 to right now.

continuo   A Baroque tradition in which the bass line is played "continuously," by a cello, double bass, and/or bassoon while a keyboard instrument (harpsichord, organ) plays the bass line and indicated harmonies.

contrapuntal   See counterpoint.

counterpoint   The combination of simultaneous parts; *see* polyphony.

crescendo   (*cresc.*) (kreh-SHEN-doh) [It.] To gradually become louder. ◁

cued notes   Smaller notes indicating either optional harmony or notes from another voice part. ♩

cut time   2/2 time with the half note getting the beat. (¢)

D

da capo   (*D.C.*) (dah KAH-poh) [It.] Go back to the beginning and repeat; *see also* dal segno and al fine.

dal segno   (*D.S.*) (dahl SAYN-yoh) [It.] Go back to the sign and repeat. (𝄋)

D. C. al fine   (dah KAH-poh ahl FEE-neh) [It.] Repeat back to the beginning and end at the "fine."

decrescendo   (*decresc.*) (deh-kreh-SHEN-doh) [It.] To gradually become softer. ⊏⊐

delicato   Delicate; to play or sing delicately.

descant   A high, ornamental voice part often lying above the melody.

diaphragm   The muscle that separates the chest cavity (thorax) from the abdomen. The primary muscle in the inhalation/exhalation cycle.

diction   Clear and correct enunciation.

diminished   The term describing an interval that has been decreased by half steps; for example, the *perfect fourth* (3 whole and one half steps) becomes a *diminished fourth* (3 whole steps). Also used for a triad which has a minor third (R, 3) and a diminished fifth (R, 5); for example, C, E♭, G♭.

diminuendo   (*dim.*) (duh-min-yoo-WEN-doh) [It.] Gradually getting softer; *see also* decrescendo.

diminution   The halving of values; that is, halves become quarters, quarters become eighths, etc. Opposite of *augmentation*.

diphthong   A combination of two vowel sounds consisting of a primary vowel sound and a secondary vowel sound. The secondary vowel sound is (usually) at the very end of the diphthong; for example, in the word *toy*, the diphthong starts with the sound of "o," then moves on to "y," in this case pronounced "ee."

dissonance   Discord in music, suggesting a state of tension or "seeking"; chords using seconds, fourths, fifths, and sevenths; the opposite of consonance.

divisi   (*div.*) (dih-VEE-see) [It.] Divide; the parts divide.

dolce   (DOHL-chay) [It.] Sweet; *dolcissimo*, very sweet; *dolcemente*, sweetly.

dominant   The fifth degree of a major or minor scale; the triad built on the fifth degree; indicated as V in harmonic analysis.

Dorian mode   A scale with the pattern of whole-step, half, whole, whole, whole, half, and whole. For example, D to D on the keyboard.

dotted rhythm   A note written with a dot increases its value again by half.

double bar   Two vertical lines placed on the staff indicating the end of a section or a composition; used with two dots to enclose repeated sections.

double flat (♭♭) Symbol showing the lowering of a pitch one whole step (two half steps).

double sharp (𝄪) Symbol showing the raising of a pitch one whole step (two half steps).

doubling   The performance of the same note by two parts, either at the same pitch or an octave apart.

downbeat   The accented first beat in a measure.

D. S. al coda   (dahl SAYN-yoh ahl KOH-dah) [It.] Repeat from the symbol (𝄋) and skip to the coda when you see the sign. (⊕)

D. S. al fine   (dahl SAYN-yoh ahl FEE-neh) [It.] Repeat from the symbol (𝄋) and sing to fine or the end.

duple   Any time signature or group of beats that is a multiple of two.

duet   Composition for two performers.

dynamics   The volume of sound, the loudness or softness of a musical passage; intensity, power.

E ————————————————

enharmonic   Identical tones that are named and written differently; for example, C sharp and D flat.

ensemble   A group of musicians or singers who perform together.

enunciation   Speaking and singing words with distinct vowels and consonants.

espressivo   (*espress.*) (es-preh-SEE-vo) [It.] For expression; *con espressione*, with feeling.

ethnomusicology   The musical study of specific world cultures.

expressive singing   To sing with feeling.

exuberance   Joyously unrestrained and enthusiastic.

F ————————————————

fermata   (fur-MAH-tah) [It.] A hold; to hold the note longer. (⌒)

fine   (FEE-neh) Ending; to finish.

flat   Symbol (accidental) that lowers a pitch by one half step. (♭)

folk music   Uncomplicated music that speaks directly of everyday matters; the first popular music; usually passed down through the oral tradition.

form   The structure of a musical composition.

forte   (*f*) (FOR-teh) [It.] Loud.

fortissimo   (*ff*) (for-TEE-suh-moh) [It.] Very loud.

freely   A direction that permits liberties with tempo, dynamics, and style.

fugue   (FYOOG) [It.] A polyphonic composition consisting of a series of successive melody imitations; *see also* imitative style.

fusion   A combination or blending of different genres of music.

G

gapped scale A scale resulting from leaving out certain tones (the pentatonic scale is an example).

grandioso [It.] Stately, majestic.

grand staff Two staves usually linked together by a long bar line and a bracket.

grave (GRAH-veh) [It.] Slow, solemn.

grazioso (grah-tsee-OH-soh) [It.] Graceful.

H

half step The smallest distance (interval) between two notes on a keyboard; the chromatic scale is composed entirely of half steps, shown as (∨).

half time *See* cut time.

harmonic interval Intervals that are sung or played simultaneously; *see also* melodic interval.

harmony Vertical blocks of different tones sounded simultaneously.

hemiola (hee-mee-OH-lah) [Gk.] A metric flow of two against a metric flow of three.

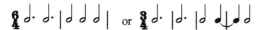

homophonic (hah-muh-FAH-nik) [Gk.] A texture where all parts sing similar rhythm in unison or harmony.

homophony (hah-MAH-fuh-nee) [Gk.] Music that consists of two or more voice parts with similar or identical rhythms. From the Greek words meaning "same sounds," homophony could be described as "hymn-style."

hushed A style marking indicating a soft, whispered tone.

I

imitation, imitative style Restating identical or nearly identical musical material in two or more parts.

improvised Invented on the spur of the moment.

improvisation Spontaneous musical invention, commonly associated with jazz.

interval The distance from one note to another; intervals are measured by the total steps and half steps between the two notes.

intonation The degree to which pitch is accurately produced in tune.

introduction An opening section at the beginning of a movement or work, preparatory to the main body of the form.

inversion May be applied to melody and harmony: *melodic inversion* occurs in an exchange of ascending and descending movement (for instance, a third becomes a sixth, a fourth becomes a fifth, etc.); *harmonic inversion* occurs in the position of the chord tones (that is, root position with the root as lowest tone, first inversion with the third as lowest tone, and second inversion with the fifth as the lowest tone).

K

key The way tonality is organized around a tonal center; *see also* key signature.

key change Changing an initial key signature in the body of a composition.

key signature Designation of sharps or flats at the beginning of a composition to indicate its basic scale and tonality.

L

leading tone The seventh degree of a scale, so called because of its strong tendency to resolve upward to the tonic.

legato (leh-GAH-toh) [It.] Smooth, connected style.

ledger lines Short lines that appear above, between treble and bass clefs, or below the bass clef, used to expand the notation.

leggiero (leh-JEH-roh) [It.] Articulate lightly; sometimes nonlegato.

lento Slow; a little faster than *largo*, a little slower than *adagio*.

linear flow, line Singing/playing notes in a flowing (smooth) manner, as if in a horizontal line.

liturgical Pertaining to prescribed forms of worship or ritual in various religious services. Western music contains much literature written for the liturgy of the early Roman Catholic Church.

lullaby A cradle song; in Western music, usually sung with a gentle and regular rhythm.

M

madrigal A secular vocal form in several parts, popular in the Renaissance.

maestoso (mah-eh-STOH-soh) [It.] Perform majestically.

major (key, scale, mode) Scale built on the formula of two whole steps, one half step, three whole steps, one half step.

Letter Names:	G	A	B	C	D	E	F♯	G
Movable Do:	do	re	mi	fa	so	la	ti	do
Numbers:	1	2	3	4	5	6	7	1

Major 2nd The name for an interval of one whole step or two half steps. For example, from C to D.

Major 6th The name for an interval of four whole steps and one-half step. For example, from C to A.

Major 3rd The name for an interval of two whole steps or four half steps. For example, from C to E.

major triad Three tones that form a major third *do* to *mi* and a minor third *mi* to *so* as in C E G.

marcato (mahr-KAH-toh) [It.] Long but separated pitches; translated as marked.

mass The main religious service of the Roman Catholic Church. There are two divisions of mass: the Proper of the Mass in which the text changes for each day, and the Ordinary of the Mass in which the text remains the same for every mass. Music for the mass includes the Kyrie, Gloria, Credo, Sanctus, and Agnus Dei as well as other chants, hymns, and psalms. For special mass occasions composers through the centuries have created large musical works for choruses, soloists, instrumentalists, and orchestras.

measure The space from one bar line to the next; also called bars.

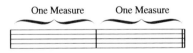

medieval Historical period prior to the Renaissance, c. 500-1450.

medley A group of tunes, linked together and sung consecutively.

melisma (n.) or melismatic (adj.) (muh-LIZ-mah or muh-liz-MAT-ik) [Gk.] A term describing the setting of one syllable of text to several pitches.

son, e - le - - i - son. _____
us, On - us - - mer - cy. _____

melodic interval Intervals that are performed in succession; *see also* harmonic interval.

melody A logical succession of musical tones; also called tune.

meter The pattern into which a steady succession of rhythmic pulses (beats) is organized.

meter signature The divided number at the beginning of a clef; 4/4, 3/4, and so forth; *see also* time signature.

metronome marking A sign that appears over the top line of the treble clef staff at the beginning of a piece indicating the tempo. It shows the kind of note that will get the beat and the numbers of beats per minute as measured by a metronome; for example, ♪ = 100.

mezzo forte (*mf*) (MEHT-soh FOR-teh) [It.] Medium loud.

mezzo piano (*mp*) (MEHT-soh pee-AH-noh) [It.] Medium soft.

mezzo voce (MET-soh VOH-cheh) [It.] With half voice; reduced volume and tone.

middle C The note that is located nearest the center of the piano keyboard; middle C can be written in either the treble or bass clef.

minor (key, scale) Scale built on the formula of one whole step, one half step, two whole steps, one half step, two whole steps.

Letter Names:	D	E	F	G	A	B♭	C	D
Movable Do:	la	ti	do	re	mi	fa	so	la
Numbers:	6	7	1	2	3	4	5	6

minor mode One of two modes upon which the basic scales of Western music are based, the other being major; using W for a whole step and H for a half step, a minor scale has the pattern W H W W H W W.

minor triad Three tones that form a minor third (bottom) and a major third (top), such as A C E.

minor third The name for an interval of three half steps. For example, from A to C.

mixed meter Frequently changing time signatures or meters.

moderato Moderate.

modulation Adjusting to a change of keys within a song.

molto Very or much; for example, *molto rit.* means "much slower."

monophonic (mah-nuh-FAH-nik) [Gk.] A musical texture having a single melodic line with no accompaniment; monophony.

monophony   (muh-NAH-fuh-nee) [Gk.] One sound; music that has a single melody. Gregorian chants or plainsongs exhibit monophony.

motet   Originating as a Medieval and Renaissance polyphonic song, this choral form of composition became an unaccompanied work, often in contrapuntal style.

motive   A shortened expression, sometimes contained within a phrase.

musical variations   Changes in rhythm, pitch, dynamics, style, and tempo to create new statements of the established theme.

mysterioso   Perform in a mysterious or haunting way; to create a haunting mood.

N

nationalism   Patriotism; pride of country. This feeling influenced many Romantic composers such as Wagner, Tchaikovsky, Dvořák, Chopin, and Brahms.

natural   (♮) Cancels a previous sharp (♯) lowering the pitch a half step, or a previous flat (♭), raising the pitch a half step.

no breath mark   A direction not to take a breath at a specific place in the composition. (🎵 or N.B.)

non-harmonic tones   Identifies those pitches outside the harmonic structure of the chord; for example, the *passing tone* and the *appoggiatura*.

non troppo   (nahn TROH-poh) [It.] Not too much; for example, allegro non troppo, not too fast.

notation   Written notes, symbols, and directions used to represent music within a composition.

nuance   Subtle variations in tempo, phrasing, dynamics, etc., to enhance the musical performance.

O

octave   An interval of twelve half steps; 8 or 8va = an octave above; 8vb = an octave below.

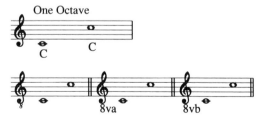

One Octave

opera   A combination of singing, instrumental music, dancing, and drama that tells a story.

operetta   A lighter, "popular" style of operatic form, including sung and spoken dialogue, solo, chorus, and dance.

optional divisi   (*opt. div.*) Indicating a split in the music into optional harmony, shown by the smaller cued note.

opus, Op.   The term, meaning "work," used by composers to show the chronological order of their works; for example, Opus 1, Op. 2.

oratorio   A piece for solo voices, chorus, and orchestra, that is an expanded dramatic work on a literary or religious theme presented without theatrical action.

ostinato   (ahs-tuh-NAH-toh) [It.] A rhythmic or melodic passage that is repeated continuously.

overtones   The almost inaudible higher pitches which occur over the fundamental tone, resulting from the division of the vibrating cycle into smaller segments; compare to partials, harmonics.

P

palate   The roof of the mouth; the *hard palate* is forward, the *soft palate* (*velum*) is at the back.

parallel major and minor keys   Major and minor keys having the same tonic, such as A major and A minor (A major being the parallel major of A minor and A minor the parallel minor of A major).

parallel motion   The movement of two or more voice parts in the same direction, at the same interval from each other.

peak   The high point in the course of a development; for example, the high point of a musical phrase or the high point in a movement of instrumental music.

pentatonic scale   A five-tone scale constructed of *do, re, mi, so, la* (degrees 1, 2, 3, 5, 6) of a corresponding major scale.

Perfect 5th   The name for an interval of three whole steps and one half step. For example, C to G.

Perfect 4th   The name for an interval of two whole steps and one half step. For example, C to F.

phrase   A musical sentence containing a beginning, middle, and end.

phrase mark   In music, an indicator of the length of a phrase in a melody; this mark may also mean that the singer or musician should not take a breath for the duration of the phrase. (‿‿‿‿)

phrasing   The realization of the phrase structure of a work; largely a function of a performer's articulation and breathing.

pianissimo   (***pp***) (pee-uh-NEE-suh-moh) [It.] Very soft.

piano   (***p***) (pee-ANN-noh) [It.] Soft.

Picardy third   An interval of a major third used in the final, tonic chord of a piece written in a minor key.

pick-up   *See* upbeat.

pitch   Sound, the result of vibration; the highness or lowness of a tone, determined by the number of vibrations per second.

piu   (pew) [It.] More; for example, *piu forte* means "more loudly."

poco   (POH-koh) [It.] Little; for example, *poco dim.* means "a little softer."

poco a poco   (POH-koh ah POH-koh) [It.] Little by little; for example, *poco a poco cresc.* means "little by little increase in volume."

polyphony (n.) or polyphonic (adj.)   (pah-LIH-fuh-nee or pah-lee-FAH-nik) [Gk.] The term that means that each voice part begins at a different place, is independent and important, and that sections often repeat in contrasting dynamic levels. Poly = many, phony = sounds.

polyrhythmic   The simultaneous use of contrasting rhythmic figures.

presto   (PREH-stoh) [It.] Very fast.

program music   A descriptive style of music composed to relate or illustrate a specific incident, situation, or drama; the form of the piece is often dictated or influenced by the nonmusical program. This style commonly occurs in music composed during the Romantic period. For example, "The Moldau" from *Má Vlast*, by Bedrich Smetana.

progression   A succession of two or more pitches or chords; also melodic or harmonic progression.

R

rallentando   (*rall.*) (rahl-en-TAHN-doh) [It.] Meaning to "perform more and more slowly." *See also* ritardando.

recitative   (res-uh-TAY-teev) [It.] A speechlike style of singing used in opera, oratorio, and cantata.

register, vocal   A term used for different parts of a singer's range, such as head register (high notes) and chest register (low notes).

relative major and minor keys   The relative minor of any major key or scale, while sharing its key signature and pitches, takes for its tonic the sixth scale degree of that major key or scale. For example, in D major the sixth scale degree is B (or *la* in solfège), *la* then becomes the tonic for A minor.

D major   B minor

Renaissance period   The historic period in Western Europe from c. 1430 to 1600; the term means "rebirth" or "renewal"; it indicates a period of rapid development in exploration, science, art, and music.

repeat sign   A direction to repeat the section of music (); if the first half of this sign is omitted, it means to "go back to the beginning" ( ).

repetition   The restatement of a musical idea; repeated pitches; repeated "A" section in ABA form.

resolution   (*res.*) A progression from a dissonant tone or harmony to a consonant harmony; a sense of completion.

resonance   Reinforcement and intensification of sound by vibrations.

rest   Symbols used to indicated silence.

rhythm   The pattern of sounds and silences.

rhythmic motif   A rhythmic pattern that is repeated throughout a movement or composition.

ritardando   (*rit.*) The gradual slowing of tempo; also called "ritard."

Rococo   Music of the Baroque period so elaborate it was named after a certain type of fancy rock work.

Romantic period   A historic period starting c. 1820 and ending c. 1900 in which artists and composers attempted to break with classical music ideas.

rondo form   An instrumental form based on an alternation between a repeated (or recurring) section and contrasting episodes (ABACADA).

root   The bottom note of a triad in its original position; the note on which the chord is built.

round   A composition in which the perpetual theme (sometimes with harmonic parts) begins in one group and is strictly imitated in other groups in an overlapping fashion. Usually the last voice to enter becomes the final voice to complete the song.

rubato   (roo-BAH-toh) [It.] Freely; allows the conductor or the performer to vary the tempo.

S

sacred music   Of or dealing with religious music; hymns, chorales, early masses; *see* secular music.

scale   A pattern of pitches arranged by whole steps and half steps.

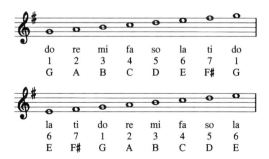

do	re	mi	fa	so	la	ti	do
1	2	3	4	5	6	7	1
G	A	B	C	D	E	F♯	G

la	ti	do	re	mi	fa	so	la
6	7	1	2	3	4	5	6
E	F♯	G	A	B	C	D	E

score The arrangement of instrumental and vocal staffs that all sound at the same time.

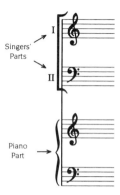

secular music Music without religious content; *see* sacred music.

sempre (SEHM-preh) [It.] Always, continually.

seventh chord By adding a seventh above the root of a triad (R, 3, 5), the result is a four-tone chord (R, 3, 5, 7).

sforzando (*sfz*) (sfohr-TSAHN-doh) [It.] A sudden strong accent on a note or chord.

sharp A symbol (accidental) that raises a pitch by one half step. (♯)

sight-sing Reading and singing of music at first sight.

simile (*sim.*) (SIM-ee-leh) [It.] To continue in the same way.

simple meter Meter in which each beat is divisible by 2.

skip Melodic movement in intervals larger than a whole step.

slur Curved line placed over or under a group of notes to indicate that they are to be performed without a break. (♩ ♩)

solfège (SOHL-fehj) [Fr.] A method of sight-singing, using the syllables *do, re, mi, fa, so, la, ti,* etc. for pitches of the scale.

solo Composition for one featured performer.

sonata-allegro form (suh-NAH-tuh ah-LEH-groh) [It.] Large A B A form consisting of three sections: exposition, development, and recapitulation.

soprano The higher female voice.

sostenuto (SAHS-tuh-noot-oh) [It.] The sustaining of a tone or the slackening of tempo; the right pedal of a piano, which, when depressed, allows the strings to vibrate.

sotto voce In a quiet, subdued manner; "under" the voice.

spirito (SPEE-ree-toh) [It.] Spirited; for example, *con spirito*, with spirit.

spiritual A type of song created by African Americans who combined African rhythms with melodies they created and heard in America.

staccato (stah-KAH-toh) [It.] Performed in a short, detached manner, as opposed to legato.

staff Series of five horizontal lines and four spaces on which music is written to show pitch.

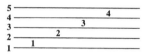

staggered entrances Voice parts or instruments begin singing or playing at different points within the composition.

steady beat A metrical pulse; *see also* beat, meter, rhythm.

step Melodic movement from one note to the next adjacent note, either higher or lower.

stepwise melodic movement Motion from one note to an adjacent one.

stress Emphasis on certain notes or rhythmic elements.

strong beat Naturally accented beats; beats 1 and 3 in 4/4 meter, beat 1 in 3/4 meter.

strophic Description of a song in which all the stanzas of the text are sung to the same music; opposite of *through-composed*.

style The particular character of a musical work; often indicated by words at the beginning of a composition, telling the performer the general manner in which the piece is to be performed.

subito (sub.) (SOO-bee-toh) [It.] Suddenly; for example, *sub. piano* means "suddenly soft."

suspension or suspended tone The tone or tones in a chord that are held as the remainder of the notes change to a new chord. The sustained tones often form a *dissonance* with the new chord, into which they then resolve.

sustained tone A tone sustained in duration; sometimes implying a slowing of tempo; *sostenuto* or *sostenendo*, abbreviated *sost*.

swing This is a performance style in which a pair of eighth notes (♫) are no longer performed evenly, but instead like a triplet (♫), yet they are still written (⌐3⌐ ♩♪); usually indicated at the beginning of a song or a section.

symphony An extended work in several movements, for orchestra; also an orchestra configured to perform symphonic music.

syncopation Deliberate shifts of accent so that a rhythm goes against the steady beat; sometimes referred to as the "offbeat."

T

tactus (TAKT-us) [Lt.] The musical term for "beat" in the fifteenth and sixteenth century; generally related to the speed of the human heart.

tempo A pace with which music moves, based on the speed of the underlying beat.

tempo I or tempo primo Return to the first tempo.

tenor A high male voice, lower than the alto, but higher than bass.

tenuto (teh-NOO-toh) [It.] Stress and extend the marked note. (𝄐)

text Words, usually set in a poetic style, that express a central thought, idea, moral, or narrative.

texture The thickness of the different layers of horizontal and vertical sounds.

theme and variation form A musical form in which variations of the basic theme comprise the composition.

tie A curved line connecting two successive notes of the same pitch, indicating that the second note is not to be articulated. (♩‿♩)

timbre Tone color; the unique quality produced by a voice or instrument.

time signature The sign placed at the beginning and within a composition to indicate the meter; for example, 4/4, 3/4; *see also* cut time, meter signature.

to coda Skip to the ⊕ or CODA.

tonality The organized relationships of pitches with reference to a definite key center. In Western music, most tonalities are organized by the major and minor scales.

tone A sound quality of a definite pitch.

tone color, quality, or timbre That which distinguishes the voice or tone of one singer or instrument from another; for example, a soprano from an alto or a flute from a clarinet.

tonic chord (TAH-nik kord) [Gk.] The name of a chord built on the tonal center of a scale; for example, C E G or *do, mi, so* for C major.

tonic or tonal center The most important pitch in a scale; *do*; the home tone; the tonal center or root of a key or scale.

tonic triad A three-note chord comprising root, third, and fifth; for example, C E G.

transposition The process of changing the key of a composition.

treble clef The symbol that appears at the beginning of the staff used for higher voices, instruments, or the piano right hand; generally referring to pitches above middle C, it wraps around the line for G, therefore it is also called the G-clef. 𝄞

triad A three-note chord built in thirds above a root tone.

trill A rapid change between the marked note and the one above it within the same key. (𝄽)

triplet A group of notes in which three notes of equal duration are sung in the time normally given to two notes of equal duration.

troppo (TROHP-oh) [It.] Too much; for example, *allegro non troppo*, not too fast.

troubadour A wandering minstrel of noble birth in southern France, Spain, and Italy during the eleventh to thirteenth centuries.

tuning The process of adjusting the tones of voices or instruments so they will sound the proper pitches.

tutti (TOO-tee) [It.] Meaning "all" or "together."

twelve-tone music Twentieth-century system of writing music in which the twelve tones of the chromatic scale are arranged into a tone row (numbered 1 to 12), and then the piece is composed by arranging and rearranging the "row" in different ways; for example, backward, forward, or in clusters of three or four pitches.

U

unison Voice parts or instruments sounding the same pitches in the same rhythm simultaneously.

upbeat A weak beat preceding the downbeat.

V

variation *See* theme and variation form, musical variations.

vivace (vee-VAH-chay) [It.] Very fast; lively.

voice crossing (or voice exchange) When one voice "crosses" above or below another voice part.

W

whole step The combination of two successive half steps. (⊔)

whole tone scale A scale consisting only of whole steps.

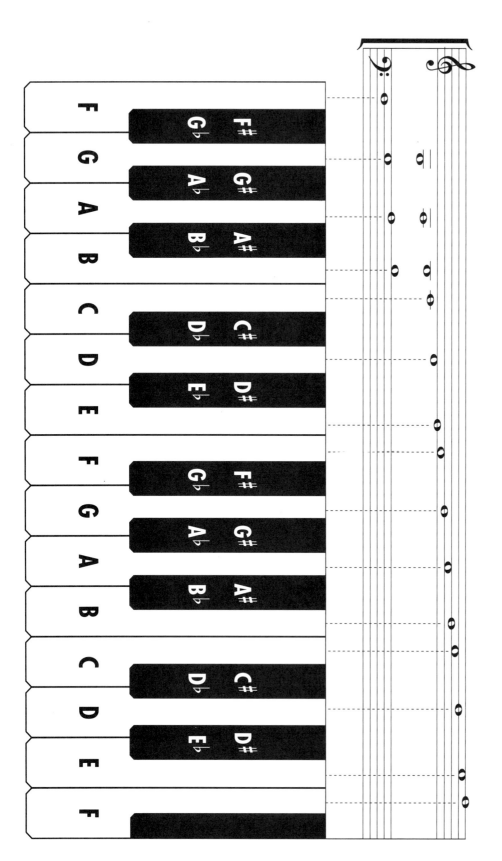